MEETING [GOD] in Scripture

Understanding
SPIRITUAL GIFTS

MEETING
[GOD]
in Scripture

—— *Understanding* ——
SPIRITUAL GIFTS

PARTICIPANT'S
WORKBOOK

Meeting God in Scripture
Understanding Spiritual Gifts Participant's Workbook
Copyright © 2010 by Upper Room Books®
All rights reserved.

No part of this book may be reproduced in any manner whatsoever without permission except in the case of brief quotations embodied in critical articles or reviews. For information, write: Upper Room Books®, 1908 Grand Avenue, Nashville, Tennessee 37212.

The Upper Room® Web site http://www.upperroom.org

UPPER ROOM®, UPPER ROOM BOOKS®, and design logos are trademarks owned by The Upper Room®, a ministry of GBOD®, Nashville, Tennessee. All rights reserved.

The Bible book introductions, the entry points, and the articles "Reading Scripture Devotionally," "What Is Spiritual Formation?" "Meeting God in Service," "Meeting God in Community," and "Meeting God in Everyday Life" originally appeared in *The Spiritual Formation Bible*, New Revised Standard Version, copyright © 1999 by The Zondervan Company. All rights reserved. This Bible is currently available as *The Meeting God Bible* (Upper Room Books).

The Spiritual Gifts Inventory Statements, Key, and Definitions were developed by Dan R. Dick. Copyright © 2001 Discipleship Resources. Used by permission.

Unless otherwise stated, scripture quotations are from the New Revised Standard Version Bible, copyright © 1989 by the Division of Christian Education of the National Council of the Churches of Christ in the U.S.A. Used by permission. All rights reserved.

Cover design: Anderson Design Group
Cover photos: © Shutterstock Images LLC, iStock International Inc., Photos.com
Interior implementation: PerfecType, Nashville, TN
First printing: 2010

ISBN: 978-0-8358-1015-9

Printed in the United States of America

Contents

INTRODUCTION	7
READING SCRIPTURE DEVOTIONALLY	11
WHAT IS SPIRITUAL FORMATION?	15
SESSIONS	
Introductory Session Shaped by God	20
Session 1 To Equip the Saints	21
Session 2 On Stage and Behind the Scenes	29
Session 3 Beyond the Lists of "Ordinary" Gifts	37
Session 4 Till All Come to Maturity	45
Session 5 With a Little Help from My Friends	53
Session 6 Not Hearers Only	61
MEETING GOD IN SERVICE	69
MEETING GOD IN COMMUNITY	73
MEETING GOD IN EVERYDAY LIFE	77
INTRODUCTIONS TO ACTS, FIRST CORINTHIANS, EPHESIANS, COLOSSIANS	81
SPIRITUAL GIFTS INVENTORY STATEMENTS AND KEY	85
SPIRITUAL GIFTS INVENTORY SCORE SHEET	93
SPIRITUAL GIFTS DEFINITIONS	94

Introduction

Welcome to *Meeting God in Scripture: Understanding Spiritual Gifts.* Over the next six weeks, we will be exploring passages in the Bible that mention or illustrate use of various spiritual gifts. This is not an exhaustive (or exhausting) study that sets out to cover every scripture verse about spiritual gifts. Within the small group and as you read the Bible at home, you will be guided to respond personally to short scripture passages. Along the way, you will also identify your gifts and consider how God wants you to use them.

[WHERE DOES YOUR "DEEP GLADNESS" MEET THE WORLD'S "DEEP HUNGER"?]

Our spiritual gifts naturally guide us toward God's will for us because they grow from within us and because we feel truly alive as we use them. The more we express them through actions, the more fully we become who God has created us to be.

Frederick Buechner says, "The place God calls you to is the place where your deep gladness and the world's deep hunger meet."* Using your gifts helps both to nourish that "deep gladness" and to bring God's power into the world in life-giving ways.

Because our spiritual gifts are sometimes more obvious to others than they are to us, people in our community of faith often name our gifts before we're aware of them. How many of us have heard something like, "You're so good at hospitality!" or, "You have a way with kids" (or "words" or "organizing") and been surprised? ***As you discuss the scripture passages over the next weeks, you will inevitably notice and perhaps hear about the talents, loves, and skills of others.*** Each week in this participant's workbook you will find a reminder to write down anything you notice about what others love and love to do. Receiving affirmation of our gifts and of using them is a catalyst for growth. Others need your insights and encouragement.

You will read thirty passages, one per day for five days during each of the next six weeks. Each reading is accompanied by an entry point that focuses on a few verses from the day's passage. These entry points are simply suggested ways you may enter

---

*Frederick Buechner, *Wishful Thinking: A Theological ABC* (New York: Harper & Row, 1973), 59.

personally into the Bible's message. The daily readings and entry-point activities will facilitate personal reflection on your interests, preferences, and talents. These activities will require no more than ten to fifteen minutes daily. At the end of each week, you will meet with others to reflect on the session's readings and entry points. ***One entry point in each session has two stars (**) beside the day.*** Even if you don't have time to do all the readings and responses, try to find time to do this one; it will be used in some way during the weekly meeting. No other preparation for the group meeting is necessary.

This book includes space for your responses to the entry points. Bring it and your Bible with you to the weekly sessions. The leader will tell you about time, place, and format for these meetings.

IF YOU WANT TO DO MORE: KEEPING A SPIRITUAL JOURNAL

Keeping a personal journal is a Christian practice that helps seekers attend to God's presence and work in daily life and events. If you have more time to give to this study each day or some days, you may want to write briefly in a journal about your prayers or other responses to the scripture readings. A journal can be a spiral-bound notebook; a file on your computer; or a slightly fancier, bound, blank book that you can find in most bookstores. The journal and what you write in it are private, between you and God. If you keep a journal, bring it with you to group meetings, since you may want to record your responses to some of the group activities. However, ***you will never be asked to reveal the contents of your journal to others***; it will remain completely private unless you choose to talk about its contents as part of group discussions.

WHAT GOES IN A JOURNAL?

Anything that you put into your journal is fine. After all, it is yours. You may write a prayer in response to a scripture reading. You may want to draw a picture of some image the reading brings to mind, or you may want to record an idea or insight that you hope to remember. You may write about connections you sense between the Bible's words and your life. If you need help finding something to write about, here are some general questions you can use to journal in response to scripture reading:

- What picture of God do I see in this passage?

- What does this passage tell me about human nature?

- What does this passage reveal about God's ways of dealing with us?

- What connection do I sense between this passage and my life right now?

- What feelings and memories arise as I reflect on this passage?

- What questions does this passage raise for me?

- How does this passage suggest that I might pray?

- What other response does this passage ask of me?

You may copy these questions into the front of your journal. After a while, you will probably find that you don't need the questions because your journal has become like a friend you can talk to easily.

If you're a first-time journaler, **don't make writing in it a task that has to be done every day**, something to feel guilty about not doing, or something that you worry about doing correctly. Even if you write only half a page a week or a month, by the end of the study you will have several pages that you otherwise would not have at all. The value of a spiritual journal is that it helps you pay attention to God. It is not an end in itself.

Reading Scripture Devotionally

The moment we open a book, a powerful set of habitual practices begins to work. Our culture teaches us learning methods that establish the reader as the controlling power who seeks to master the text in order to use it for his or her own purposes. The cognitive, analytical aspects of our beings are hyperdeveloped in our culture; we tend to think that the sharper we are intellectually, the smarter we are; the more quickly we grasp concepts and synthesize them, the more balanced we are.

Responding to God with our whole being entails loving God with all of our mind and using our cognitive abilities. We cannot shirk this aspect. Jesus, however, puts loving God with the heart and soul higher on his list: "'Love the Lord your God with all your heart and with all your soul and with all your mind'" (Matt. 22:37). Loving God with heart and soul precedes loving God with mind. Listing "mind" last doesn't make it less important but implies that it is not the only way to respond to God—or even the dominant way to respond as our culture asserts. (All three synoptic Gospels [see Mark 12:30; Luke 10:27] employ the same order.)

> LOVING GOD WITH HEART AND SOUL PRECEDES LOVING GOD WITH MIND.

CHARACTERISTICS OF FORMATIONAL SCRIPTURE READING

Our culture's predominant mode of response, however, is often the rational, cognitive, and intellectual. ***When this mind-set becomes our only mode of reading scripture, we may find it difficult to have "ears to hear"*** (Mark 4:9, 23; Luke 8:8; 14:35). When the mind is our primary filter for scripture, our approach can create an imbalance. We can easily read scripture in a purely cognitive way and decide that this passage doesn't apply to us. (We frequently even pick out some other troublesome person who should obviously heed this text instead of ourselves!) This purely cognitive way of reading insulates the "door" of our being against God's "knocking." Why? We are not really opening our being at deeper levels to the possibility of meeting God in that passage.

What if God wishes to meet us in the passage in an intimate way, according to God's wisdom, communicating what we need to hear but wish to avoid? Allowing God's word to speak transformationally to the deepest levels of our being invites us to develop another way of reading.

FORMATIONAL SCRIPTURE READING

Formational scripture reading differs from our usual approach. Formational scripture reading invites us to open ourselves, allowing God to set the agenda for our lives through the text. It facilitates genuine spiritual formation—the process of being conformed to the image of Jesus Christ. **Reading formationally helps us open our "rational filter," which can sift out so much of God's voice.** We begin to hear at the heart-and-soul level. Jesus frequently reminded people of the importance of having "ears to hear" (Mark 4:9, 23; Luke 8:8; 14:35).

Formational reading can help us develop those ears to hear. Let me share a personal experience of formational reading. I was following a prescribed plan for Bible reading and had come to the Exodus event. I'd read about the struggle between God and Pharaoh many times but only informationally. As I read the daily assigned portion, I sat before it and said, **"Lord, what are you seeking to say to me through this?"** All sorts of thoughts went through my mind—who said what, Pharaoh's resistance, God's hardening Pharaoh's heart. I got nothing from the text after wrestling with it for a week or more. Finally, each day's portion moved one by one through the ten plagues. I was met each time with silence—or my own noisy understanding of the passage. As I moved toward the end of the passage about the plagues and asked that same question, an answer came: "You are Pharaoh!" "What?" I replied. "Me, Pharaoh? Moses, perhaps, even one of the Hebrews, but Pharaoh? Perhaps a servant or slave, but Pharaoh?" Possibilities began to open up in the text and inside me. I realized that God had given me certain gifts, abilities, and personality traits. All these were God's "children," but I had enslaved them to my own purposes, desires, intentions, and plans. Truly I was the Pharaoh of my life! I came to the last plague—the death of the firstborn. I saw that for me to cease to be Pharaoh in my life, there had to be a death of my "firstborn" desires to use God's gifts for my own purposes. To liberate those gifts for God's use in my life, I would have to cease to be Pharaoh.

CHARACTERISTICS OF FORMATIONAL SCRIPTURE READING

Depth. Informational reading seeks to cover as much material as possible as quickly as possible, while formational reading involves smaller portions of scripture. The point is not just to get through the text but to become personally involved in it. Formational reading is concerned with depth, so we may find ourselves "holding on" to just one sentence or paragraph or page for quite a while. We allow the passage to open out to us its deeper dynamics and multiple layers of meaning. **We let the text intrude into our life and address us.**

Openness. In formational reading, **we let the text master us**. We come to the text with an openness to hear, to receive, and to respond. This may feel risky because it lays us open to unforeseen conclusions.

Humility. Formational reading requires a humble approach, a new inner posture in which we willingly relinquish our insights and purposes. We stand before scripture and await its address.

Mystery. Informational reading can be characterized by a problem-solving mentality. When we do respond, we often read our needs and desires into the scripture, asking, **Does this passage solve my problems, answer my questions, meet my needs?** Formational reading invites us to become open to the whole mystery of God. We allow God to address us however God wishes. Eventually, we may discover that problem-solving dynamics emerge from the encounter, but we relinquish the right to solve our problems with scripture.

SUGGESTIONS FOR FORMATIONAL SCRIPTURE READING

Make listening for God's voice a top priority. Focus your attention on what God is saying to you as you read. Listen for God to speak to you in and through, around and within, over and behind the words. Keep asking yourself, "What is God seeking to say to me in all of this?" Allow the text to become an instrument of God's voice in your life. Respond to what you read with your heart and spirit.

Let your response take place down in the deeper levels of your being. Ask yourself questions such as: How do I feel about what is being said? How am I reacting? How am I responding down deep within myself? What is going on inside of me? Then begin to ask yourself "why" questions: *Why* do I feel this way? *Why* am I responding in this manner? *Why* do I have these feelings within?

Let this exercise be **an opportunity to get in touch with the deeper layers of your being**. What do your reactions tell you about your habits, your attitudes, your perspectives, your responses, and your reactions to life? Are you beginning to see something about yourself? Thomas à Kempis said, **"A humble knowledge of ourselves is a surer way to God than is the search for depth of learning."** That humble knowledge of yourself can come when you read scripture if you balance your cognitive response pattern with this affective response from deep within your being.

Prepare to read by quieting yourself. You can't run in, sit down, pick up the text, and read scripture formationally. You have to "center down," to use the old Quaker phrase—**become still, relinquish your agenda, and acknowledge the presence of God**. You may have to relax first in order to do this. When you center yourself in this way, you may find that no word addresses you out of that text on that day, but the constant discipline of preparing yourself and entering into formational reading will itself be spiritually forming to your soul.

Allow the two kinds of reading—informational and formational—to work together. You may begin reading a scripture passage with informational dynamics, but then you must be sensitive to the need to move to the formational dynamics of reading. Allow yourself to become open and receptive to the intrusion of the living Word of God into your garbled, distorted self. You may get tripped up on an informational point and need to move back to an informational mode. There is a necessary interplay between these two approaches, but **you'll ultimately need to arrive at a disciplined development of the formational mode of approaching the text.** As we become skilled at shifting to that inner posture of becoming listeners, we develop "ears to hear." We become receptive and accessible to being addressed by the living Word of God.

—M. Robert Mulholland Jr.

What Is Spiritual Formation?

HUMAN BEINGS ARE creatures of the future. Unlike other inhabitants of creation whose lives are fixed within the boundaries of genetics and instinct, human existence is open-ended, laced with mystery, like moist clay in a potter's hand. We are works in progress, shaped by the constant rhythms of nature and the unexpected turns of history. Sometimes elated and sometimes burdened by our unfinished condition, we live our days conscious that "what we will be has not yet been made known" (1 John 3:2). A sense of our true identity always seems just beyond our grasp, always awaiting us.

Personal formation occurs as nature and history interact with pliable human existence that is rich with significant potential. *Human beings are formed by the sculpting of will, intellect, and emotion into a distinct way of being in the world.* Such formation of character will assume a wide range of expression depending on our location geographically, socially, economically, and culturally. Family values, social conventions, cultural assumptions, the turning points of an epoch, the painful secrets of a heart—these and other factors combine to form or deform the direction, depth, and boundaries of our lives. Formation is therefore a fundamental characteristic of human life. It happens whether or not we are aware of it, and its effect may as often inhibit as promote healthy, fulfilled humanity.

For people of biblical faith, nature and history of themselves are not the final sources of personal formation. Rather, they are means through which the God who formed all things molds human beings into the contours of their truest destiny: the unfettered praise of God (see Isa. 43:21). To be shaped by God's gracious design is a particular expression of personal formation—spiritual formation. Irenaeus, third-century bishop of Lyons, observed that *"the glory of God is the human being fully alive."* The God known in scripture is a God who continuously forms something out of nothing—earth and heaven, creatures great and small, a people who call upon God's name, the "inmost being" (Ps. 139:13) of every human life. Yet the majestic sweep of God's formational activity never eclipses the intimacy God desires and seeks with us. Having carefully and lovingly formed each of us in the womb, God knows us by name and will not forget us (see Isa. 43:1; 44:21, 24). In the biblical perspective, to be a person means to exist in a relationship of ongoing spiritual formation with the God whose interest extends to the roots of our being.

For Christians, the pattern and fulfillment of God's work of spiritual formation converge in a single figure—Jesus Christ. Jesus is the human being fully alive, fully open to God's work in the world. Simultaneously, Jesus is God's work fully alive, fully embodied in the world. For all who are heavily burdened and wearied by the torments of the world, for all who long to dwell in the house of the Lord, Jesus is the level way, the whole truth, and the radiant life. Christians are placed daily before the greatest of all choices: to be conformed to the luminous image of Jesus Christ through the gracious assistance of God the Holy Spirit or to be conformed to the ravaged image of the world through the deceitful encouragement of the "powers of this dark world" (Rom. 12:2; Eph. 6:10-13).

Spiritual formation in the Christian tradition, then, is a lifelong process through which our new humanity, hidden with Jesus Christ in God, becomes ever more visible and effective through the leading of the Holy Spirit. ***Spiritual formation at its best has been understood to be at once fully divine and fully human—that is, initiated by God and manifested in both vital communities of faith and in the lives of individual disciples.*** We see this theme carried through the history of the church, from Paul's introduction of formation in Jesus Christ as the central work of Christian life (Gal. 4:19) to early formational writings such as the Didache (second century); to the formative intent of monastic rules; to the shaping purpose of Protestant manuals of piety; to the affirmation of lay formation in the documents of Vatican II; and finally to the current search for practices that open us to God.

OUR NEW HUMANITY

Our unfinished character leads us to acknowledge that ***"what we will be has not yet been made known."*** Yet Christians, looking at Jesus Christ, can add with confident hope that "we shall be like him" (1 John 3:2). This hope originates in the hidden dimensions of baptism. Baptism unites us with the full sweep of Jesus' life and death, resurrection, and ascension in glory to the eternal communion of love enjoyed by our triune God.

In baptism, motifs of cleansing from the stain of sin coexist with images of death and rebirth to signal the new life we enter through this spiritual birth canal (John 3:1-6).

At the center of this rebirth from above is the Paschal mystery—*the pattern of self-relinquishment and loving availability Jesus freely manifested in his ministry and in his final journey* to Jerusalem and Golgotha. This is the mysterious pattern of God's work in the world, the pattern of loss that brings gain, willing sacrifice that yields abundance, self-forgetfulness that creates a space for the remembering God. It is the pattern that steers our course from bondage to freedom—from the ways of the old Adam, who turned and hid from the One who so lovingly formed him, *to the freedom of the new Adam*, Jesus Christ, who lives with God in unbroken intimacy.

This unfolding of baptismal grace in daily life, this passing from bondage to freedom, is spiritual formation. Because *spiritual formation draws us into the fullness of life in Jesus Christ,* it shares the qualities of Jesus Christ. Thus, spiritual formation is eminently personal yet inherently corporate: *It erases nothing of our unique humanity but transposes it into a larger reality*—the mystical body of Jesus Christ in and through which we are, as the Episcopal Book of Common Prayer notes, "very members incorporate" of one another. Spiritual formation is also fully human, reflecting our own decisions, commitments, disciplines, and actions. At the same time, *spiritual formation is wholly divine, an activity initiated by God and completed by God,* in which we have been generously embraced for the sake of the world.

THE HOLY SPIRIT'S LEADING

The sweeping movement of grace by which the world was created and is sustained is orchestrated by God the Holy Spirit. In God's sovereign freedom, the Holy Spirit stirs where the Spirit chooses. Remarkably, *the Spirit has selected human life as a privileged place of redemptive activity.* In the day-to-day rhythms of life, the Holy Spirit comes to us with gentle persistence, inviting us to join the dance of life with God. In this holy dance the Spirit takes the lead, a partner both sensitive and sure. *"The spiritual life is the life of God's Spirit in us,"* notes Marjorie Thompson, "the living interaction between our spirit and the Holy Spirit through which we mature into the full stature of Christ and become more surrendered to the work of the Spirit within and around us."

There are settings and disciplines that prepare us to recognize and respond to the Holy Spirit's invitation. The church, the body of Jesus Christ visible and tangible in the world, as rich with promise as it is with paradox—is the principal context in which to sharpen our spiritual senses. The mere fact of gathering with others on the Lord's Day reminds us that the Holy Spirit continuously draws together what evil strives to scatter. In congregational worship, we hear God's word to us; recall how lavishly God loves us; see this love enacted in baptism; taste its sweetness and its wonder in the Lord's Supper; and take stock of our response to it in confession, hymn, and corporate prayer. Small groups given to prayer, study, or outreach also offer places to increase our awareness of the Holy Spirit's leading. In the company of faithful seekers, another person's moment of vulnerability, a truth spoken in love or a story told in trust can awaken insight into ways the Holy Spirit is also present with us. Family life, which Martin Luther placed ahead of the monastery as the true school of charity, provides many opportunities to learn the art of self-forgetfulness. ***Time spent with the poor and needy instructs us in our own poverty,*** prepares us to receive more than we bestow from those who often seem so distressingly different, and gives the Spirit occasion to teach us the extent of our common humanity.

Personal spiritual practices also prime us to be responsive to the Holy Spirit's approach. The meditative reading encouraged in the Meeting God in Scripture series enables us to become at home in God's Word. As this occurs, we develop a growing familiarity with the Holy Spirit who fashioned and continues to dwell in holy writ. According to twelfth-century Cistercian abbot Peter of Celle, such reading is nothing less than "the soul's food, light, lamp, refuge, consolation, and the spice of every spiritual savor." ***Prayer, that royal road to deepening intimacy with God, will inevitably acquaint us with the guiding grace of the Spirit.*** It is in the Spirit that we pray and through the Spirit that the inarticulate yearnings of our heart receive coherent expression before God (see Rom. 8:27). Various "spiritual fitness" exercises, including abstaining from self-destructive activities and attitudes, allocating personal resources in a godly manner, and following simple rules of life, ***remind us that God is the center of each day.*** Such exercises produce stamina for continued acceptance of the Holy Spirit's invitation to "come and follow."

Following the leading of the Holy Spirit builds capacity for extraordinary witness to God's kingdom, such as extending forgiveness where there has been genuine injury.

It reinforces in us the knowledge that *our new humanity in Jesus Christ is the work of the Spirit and not our own achievement.* In our human weakness, we need the strength and sustenance of the Holy Spirit to maintain the Godward direction of our life. Such assistance is promised by Jesus: "When he, the Spirit of truth, comes, he will guide you into all truth" (John 16:13). The author of Ephesians calls this truth "the fullness of Christ" (Eph. 4:13). The measure of this truth is nothing other than love. *Love is the first gift of the Spirit and the final test of our freedom in Jesus Christ* (see 1 Cor. 13; Gal. 5:22; Col. 1:8). Other marks of our new humanity—joy, peace, patience, kindness, generosity, faithfulness, self-control—are manifestations of this love that binds us to Jesus Christ in the unity of the Holy Spirit for the sake of the world God loves so much. "Since we live by the Spirit, let us keep in step with the Spirit" (Gal. 5:25).

IN THE WORLD

In a life increasingly given to the guidance of the Holy Spirit, our new humanity in Jesus Christ gradually becomes more visible and effective in the world. Far from removing us from the messiness of the world, *spiritual formation plunges us into the middle of the world's rage and suffering.* It was to this place of pain and bewilderment that Jesus Christ was sent as the visible image of the invisible God (see John 14:9; Col. 1:15). It was to this place of bitterness and infirmity that Jesus Christ was sent, not to condemn but to save (see John 3:17). Those who are being formed in his image take the same path. Love, the full measure of Christian maturity, impels us with kindly urgency in this direction. *Love desires to be seen, known and received, for by these actions it grows wider and deeper.* Through us love is extended to the furthest recesses of human sorrow and need. Thus, God's love for the world—in us because we are in Jesus Christ—becomes a sign of hope and a source of transformation in the world.

"No one is richer, no one more powerful, no one more free," observed Thomas à Kempis, "than *the person who can give his whole life to God and freely serve others with deep humility and love.*" To embody in thought, word, and deed the love of God made known in our Lord Jesus Christ is the signal mark of faithful discipleship, the inexhaustible strength of vital congregations, and the ultimate goal of spiritual formation.

—John Mogabgab

SESSION | **INTRO**

Shaped by God

Read Genesis 1:1-31 and 2:1-8. Read again Genesis 2:7.

These passages offer us a wonderful image of the way God forms us both physically and spiritually.
As you held the clay, feeling the weight and temperature, noticing its pliability, working with it, how did you make it into a particular form? Based on this exercise, what do you think spiritual formation means? How is God molding or forming you continually, even today? How do you resist or receive God's attention? Note your thoughts on this page.

[**ENTRY POINT:** "God Forms Us"]

Genesis 2:7
Then the Lord God formed man from the dust of the ground, and breathed into his nostrils the breath of life; and the man became a living being.

I FEEL GOD IS WITH ME EVERY DAY IN EVERY WAY SO I JUST SET BACK AND LET GOD HAVE HIS WAY IN MY LIFE

SESSION ONE

To Equip the *Saints*

SESSION ONE — *Day 1* **

Read 1 Corinthians 12:1, 4-30. Read again 1 Corinthians 12:4-7.

Paul proposes that unity in diversity is central to life in the Christian community.

He sees in the community different gifts but the same Spirit; different services and deeds but the same God working through them;

[**ENTRY POINT:** **Unity in Diversity**]

an array of people called to be baptized—Jews and Greeks, slaves and free—who are part of the same body. How might the words of this passage influence the way you relate to people in the church? the way in which you pray? To bring Paul's message closer to home, name someone you know who is suffering. Think of another person who has recently been honored or acknowledged in some way. Think of someone who exhibits each of the spiritual gifts listed in verses 28 through 30.

1 Corinthians 12:4-7

Now there are varieties of gifts, but the same Spirit; and there are varieties of services, but the same Lord; and there are varieties of activities, but it is the same God who activates all of them in everyone. To each is given the manifestation of the Spirit for the common good.

PEGGY McMICHELS

JUSTIN LAROSA

SESSION ONE

Read Exodus 31:1-11. Read again Exodus 31:1-6.

Look carefully at your hands, both front and back.
Consider their shape and distinctive markings. Do you have long fingers such as the kind good for playing the piano? What scars or other evidence do you see from past "adventures" and activities? What else do your hands say about you?

[ENTRY POINT: **Helping Hands, Healing Hands**]

In the past, how have you used your hands in creative activities? in sports? in tasks that you love and in those that you hate? On a more general scale, consider the skills you have worked to develop. How might you use them in the next twenty-four hours to create, to show care, to make the world more like God wants it to be?

How might you use your hands during the next week? in the longer term?

Exodus 31:1-6

The LORD spoke to Moses: See, I have called by name Bezalel son of Uri son of Hur, of the tribe of Judah: and I have filled him with divine spirit, with ability, intelligence, and knowledge in every kind of craft, to devise artistic designs, to work in gold, silver, and bronze, in cutting stones for setting, and in carving wood, in every kind of craft. Moreover, I have appointed with him Oholiab son of Ahisamach, of the tribe of Dan; and I have given skill to all the skillful, so that they may make all that I have commanded you.

I SEE MY HANDS MORE WILLING TO HELP OTHERS WITH HOME REPAIRS

SESSION ONE — *Day 3*

Read Acts 2:1-4. Read again Acts 2:1-4.

How do you picture the Holy Spirit? Here the Spirit is likened to a violent wind and tongues of fire. In Matthew 3:16 the Spirit is compared to a descending dove.

[ENTRY POINT: **All Have Gifts**]

Elsewhere the Spirit is experienced through various gifts (see 1 Cor. 12:4-11) and fruit (see Gal. 5:22-23). Try praising God with your hands as you draw or paint your own image or images of the Spirit.

Acts 2:1-4

When the day of Pentecost had come, they were all together in one place. And suddenly from heaven there came a sound like the rush of a violent wind, and it filled the entire house where they were sitting. Divided tongues, as of fire, appeared among them, and a tongue rested on each of them. All of them were filled with the Holy Spirit and began to speak in other languages, as the Spirit gave them ability.

THE GIFTS OF THE SPIRIT, IS LOVE, JOY, PEACE, LONGSUFFERING KINDNESS, GOODNESS, FAITHFULLNESS GENTLENESS, SELF CONTROL

SESSION ONE

Read Exodus 39:2-7. Read again Exodus 39:2-7.

The careful and elaborate construction of priestly garments signified to the people that worshiping God was an awesome privilege not to be undertaken carelessly or casually; God is honored by the work of a skilled craftsperson.

[ENTRY POINT: **Workers in Skilled Craft**]

Think about your talents and gifts. What can you offer God in worship today? Might it be a song played or sung with all your heart? a few moments of your undivided attention spent in prayer? a poem that expresses your gratitude to God or a sketch that shows your appreciation for God's creation? Whatever you offer to God in worship, offer your best.

Exodus 39:2-7

He made the ephod of gold, of blue, purple, and crimson yarns, and of fine twisted linen. Gold leaf was hammered out and cut into threads to work into the blue, purple, and crimson yarns and into the fine twisted linen, in skilled design. They made for the ephod shoulder-pieces, joined to it at its two edges. The decorated band on it was of the same materials and workmanship, of gold, of blue, purple, and crimson yarns, and of fine twisted linen; as the Lord had commanded Moses.

The onyx stones were prepared, enclosed in settings of gold filigree and engraved like the engravings of a signet, according to the names of the sons of Israel. He set them on the shoulder-pieces of the ephod, to be stones of remembrance for the sons of Israel; as the Lord had commanded Moses.

SESSION ONE

Read Romans 12:4-10. Read again Romans 12:4-5.

When plants give off oxygen in photosynthesis, they provide oxygen human beings and animals need for respiration. Human beings and animals give off carbon dioxide for plants to use. This interdependence that God has built into all creation mirrors the pattern for our life in Jesus Christ. We all worship the same God and face many of the same problems, yet each of us experiences life—and God— in unique ways. Our particular perspective may provide useful insight for others to apply to their lives. Each of us belongs to others, and each of us is to offer our unique gifts and talents to help the body grow.

[ENTRY POINT: **Creator, Creation, and Call**]

What are your spiritual gifts? How do you use them as part of the body of Christ? Ask God to help you review your gifts and service. Are you mutually dependent on others in the body, or are you a "lone ranger"? In what ways can you offer yourself as a "living sacrifice" (Rom. 12:1)?

Romans 12:4-5

For as in one body we have many members, and not all the members have the same function, so we, who are many, are one body in Christ, and individually we are members one of another.

Note: What do you want to remember from this week's meeting? What did you notice about group members' gifts and passions as you talked with them and got to know them a bit (or a bit better)?

SESSION TWO

On Stage and Behind *the Scenes*

Note: No daily reading is starred this week because you will be completing the Spiritual Gifts Inventory during the weekly meeting. Your group leader will provide instructions.

SESSION TWO

Read 1 Samuel 16:11-12, 17-18. Read again 1 Samuel 16:11-12, 17-18.

Samuel has warned Saul (see 13:13-14) that the Lord will remove him as king in favor of one "after [the Lord's] own heart." Samuel is guided by the Lord in his search for the new king, learning that people look "on the outward appearance, but the Lord looks on the heart," the core of one's being (v. 7).

[ENTRY POINT: **Traits of a Leader**]

Recall a time when your evaluation of a person's character or suitability for service relied mainly on outward appearance. Did this prove to be misleading or cause problems later? Consider now how God can help you look at people rightly, as the Lord sees them. Pray about a relationship with someone in which having new eyes might make all the difference.

1 Samuel 16:11-12, 17-18

Samuel said to Jesse, "Are all your sons here?" And he said, "There remains yet the youngest, but he is keeping the sheep." And Samuel said to Jesse, "Send and bring him; for we will not sit down until he comes here." He sent and brought him in. Now he was ruddy, and had beautiful eyes, and was handsome. The Lord said, "Rise and anoint him; for this is the one." . . . So Saul said to his servants, "Provide for me someone who can play well, and bring him to me." One of the young men answered, "I have seen a son of Jesse the Bethlehemite who is skillful in playing, a man of valor, a warrior, prudent in speech, and a man of good presence; and the Lord is with him."

SESSION TWO

Read Acts 2:14-25, 37-41. Read again Acts 2:14, 37-39, 41.

After the Holy Spirit descended on the gathered disciples (Acts 2:1-4), Peter stood and spoke to the crowd. He explained the meaning of various scriptures, and because of Peter's powerful words about the scriptures and Jesus' death and resurrection, thousands became followers of Christ.

[ENTRY POINT: **The Gift of Preaching**]

Think of someone who seems to have the spiritual gift of preaching. What makes that person's preaching effective? What makes you say this?

Of course we do not all have Peter's gift, but each of us can tell others what we believe. On an index card, write a personal creed stating who you think Jesus is and three or four statements about your faith journey. Meditate on your creed so you can remember what it says, and look for opportunities in the next twenty-four hours to engage someone in conversation about Christian faith. Be ready to give reason "for the hope that is in you; yet do it with gentleness and reverence" (1 Pet. 3:15-16).

Acts 2:14, 37-39, 41

But Peter, standing with the eleven, raised his voice and addressed them, "Men of Judea and all who live in Jerusalem, let this be known to you, and listen to what I say."

Now when they heard this, they were cut to the heart and said to Peter and to the other apostles, "Brothers, what should we do?" Peter said to them, "Repent, and be baptized every one of you in the name of Jesus Christ so that your sins may be forgiven; and you will receive the gift of the Holy Spirit. For the promise is for you, for your children, and for all who are far away, everyone whom the Lord our God calls to him." So those who welcomed his message were baptized, and that day about three thousand persons were added.

SESSION TWO

Read Acts 6:1-6. Read again Acts 6:1-6.

The apostles realized that they could not do everything that needed to be done in the Christian community. (This is a lesson many of us are still trying to learn.) So they chose people to work specifically with caring for the needy, commissioning these workers by laying hands on them and praying for the Spirit to empower them.

[ENTRY POINT:
Commissoned to Care]

How does your congregation recognize and support those who work in hunger ministries, prayer ministries, congregational care, and other behind-the-scenes service? Take time within the next twenty-four hours to pray for someone involved in such serving. Write a note to express appreciation for his or her witness and convey your prayer for that individual.

Thinking now of your own life, how do you decide which activities to participate in and which not? In what activity connected with church have you remained involved over a long period of time, and why? What keeps you involved?

Acts 6:1-6

Now during those days, when the disciples were increasing in number, the Hellenists complained against the Hebrews because their widows were being neglected in the daily distribution of food. And the twelve called together the whole community of the disciples and said, "It is not right that we should neglect the word of God in order to wait on tables. Therefore, friends, select from among yourselves seven men of good standing, full of the Spirit and of wisdom, whom we may appoint to this task, while we, for our part, will devote ourselves to prayer and to serving the word." What they said pleased the whole community, and they chose Stephen, a man full of faith and the Holy Spirit, together with Philip, Prochorus, Nicanor, Timon, Parmenas, and Nicolaus, a proselyte of Antioch. They had these men stand before the apostles, who prayed and laid their hands on them.

SESSION TWO — *Day 4*

Read Acts 6:8-10. Read again Acts 6:8-10.

Filled with grace, Stephen spoke with such power that his hearers "could not withstand" his wisdom and reasoning. Several of the spiritual gifts listed in scripture might be described as "speaking" gifts. List the ones you remember that could fit in this category. Which of these gifts have you most recently witnessed being used?

[ENTRY POINT: **Speaking with Power**]

When you think of someone speaking for God with wisdom and power, who comes to mind? Is this person's gift used publicly or privately?

The number-one fear of most adults is speaking in public, so *not* being terrified of that possibility might indicate the presence of a spiritual gift God can use. Are you one of those comfortable speaking to a group or one who shies away from doing so?

Do you think you have any of the spiritual gifts related to speaking about faith? Why or why not?

Acts 6:8-10

Stephen, full of grace and power, did great wonders and signs among the people. Then some of those who belonged to the synagogue of the Freedmen (as it was called), Cyrenians, Alexandrians, and others of those from Cilicia and Asia, stood up and argued with Stephen. But they could not withstand the wisdom and the Spirit with which he spoke.

SESSION TWO

Read Genesis 4:20-21. Read again Genesis 4:20-21.

Think for a moment about your biological kin or the people in the household where you grew up.

What comes to mind as a skill, interest, or talent that many of you share? Using your surname, write three sentences, such as, "The Lees have always . . ." or, "We Smiths value . . ." or, "The Garcias believe in . . ." to describe your family.

[ENTRY POINT: **Family Traits and Traditions**]

Overall, do your statements reflect a heritage more like Jabal's (physical labor and outdoorsy pursuits) or Jubal's (fine arts and creativity, mental pursuits)? How are each of these talent clusters God's gifts?

Do you naturally tend toward physical expressions of your faith—such as feeding people, serving as an usher, or caring for the church grounds—or toward wisdom, knowledge, prayer, or other activities that might be considered spiritual? Whichever group you place yourself in, what do you see as the special contributions of those with the other tendency?

Genesis 4:20-21

Adah bore Jabal; he was the ancestor of those who live in tents and have livestock. His brother's name was Jubal; he was the ancestor of all those who play the lyre and pipe.

Note: What do you want to remember from this week's meeting? What passions, gifts, and talents did you notice in members of your group?

SESSION THREE

Beyond the Lists of "Ordinary"

Gifts

SESSION THREE *Day 1*

Read 1 Samuel 25:2-37. Read again 1 Samuel 25:32-35.

Reinhold Niebuhr wrote in *Beyond Tragedy*: "Goodness, armed with power, is corrupted; and pure love without power is destroyed."* Abigail's sensible intercession saves David from misusing his power by launching a bloodbath. As his temper subsides, David realizes that Abigail's transparent goodness has brought about this change of heart.

[ENTRY POINT: **Intercession for Peace**]

Recall one or more persons who have brought such goodness into your life, perhaps saving you from an unwise or destructive course of action. Calling upon this lived experience, make a list of the attributes of a "good person." Prudence might be one, and gentleness another; try to think of at least ten qualities. Prayerfully consider how you might cultivate such virtues.

1 Samuel 25:32-35

David said to Abigail, "Blessed be the Lord, the God of Israel, who sent you to meet me today! Blessed be your good sense, and blessed be you, who have kept me today from bloodguilt and from avenging myself by my own hand! For as surely as the Lord the God of Israel lives, who has restrained me from hurting you, unless you had hurried and come to meet me, truly by morning there would not have been left to Nabal so much as one male." Then David received from her hand what she had brought him; he said to her, "Go up to your house in peace; see, I have heeded your voice, and I have granted your petition."

**Beyond Tragedy: Essays on the Christian Interpretation of History* (New York: Charles Scribner's Sons, 1937), 185.

Beyond the Lists of "Ordinary" **GIFTS**

SESSION THREE

Read Ruth 1:5-17. Read again Ruth 1:8, 16.

Something about Naomi and Ruth's relationship made Ruth willing to leave her family and country and adopt a new faith.

[**ENTRY POINT: Spiritual Friendship**]

Think, for a moment, about your past relationships. Have you ever had a relationship with someone who was nonbiological kin but who nevertheless seemed like family? What characterizes such friendships? What friendship has made the most difference in your life?

Ruth 1:8, 16

But Naomi said to her two daughters-in-law, "Go back each of you to your mother's house. May the LORD deal kindly with you, as you have dealt with the dead and with me." . . . But Ruth said, "Do not press me to leave you or to turn back from following you! Where you go, I will go; Where you lodge, I will lodge; your people shall be my people, and your God my God."

SESSION THREE — *Day 3*

Read Numbers 4:46-49. Read again Numbers 4:46-49.

The Levites served according to their individual abilities.

For instance, only those who were physically strong were expected to carry heavy loads.

[ENTRY POINT: **Strong Backs and Servant Hearts**]

Likewise, God calls us according to our unique aptitudes. But we often overlook our more "everyday" human attributes like having a strong back or being able to repair machines or grow flowers. Some of us can organize; some can do accounting; some can greet people warmly and make them feel welcome; some can make plants grow. Think about such abilities and how God might use them. Which of your natural aptitudes and interests do you use to serve God? What skills and aptitudes are you developing for God's use in the future?

Numbers 4:46-49

All those who were enrolled of the Levites, whom Moses and Aaron and the leaders of Israel enrolled, by their clans and their ancestral houses, from thirty years old up to fifty years old, everyone who qualified to do the work of service and the work of bearing burdens relating to the tent of meeting, their enrollment was eight thousand five hundred eighty. According to the commandment of the LORD through Moses they were appointed to their several tasks of serving or carrying; thus they were enrolled by him, as the LORD commanded Moses.

Beyond the Lists of "Ordinary" **GIFTS**

SESSION THREE

Read Exodus 35:30-35. Read again Exodus 35:34-35.

Bezalel could be a kind of patron saint to artists

and other creative types. His name figures prominently, and his craftsmanship is celebrated, in this passage. While due credit is given to his coworker Oholiab, Moses obviously gives his highest praise to Bezalel. Bezalel challenges our cultural tendency to separate the secular from the sacred in the artistic realm. He is obviously gifted in arts and crafts; his example teaches us that we can pray not only with folded hands but also with busy hands. Hands that carve wood, that sweep a paintbrush across canvas, that cut stone, all give glory to God also.

[ENTRY POINT: **Skilled Artisans**]

How do you use your hands creatively? Ask our Creator to use your talents to bring good to others and honor to God.

Exodus 35:34-35

And he has inspired him to teach, both him and Oholiab son of Ahisamach, of the tribe of Dan. He has filled them with skill to do every kind of work done by an artisan or by a designer or by an embroiderer in blue, purple, and crimson yarns, and in fine linen, or by a weaver—by any sort of artisan or skilled designer.

SESSION THREE — *Day 5* * *

Read 1 Samuel 16:14-23. Read again 1 Samuel 16:16-17, 22.

Shakespeare often gets the credit, but William Congreve actually wrote the words "Music has charms to soothe a savage breast, / To soften rocks, or bend a knotted oak." When Saul is beset by an evil spirit, David's music brings him relief and peace.

[ENTRY POINT: **Sweet Music**]

What music soothes your "savage breast"? What hymns or sacred songs draw you toward a calm and peaceful trust in God? Sing such a song to yourself, or turn on background music as you read or reread this passage. What phrases or Bible verses deepen your trust in God's peace-giving power? Recite prayerfully a phrase or Bible verse, either on a single note or in a simple melody, as music of praise from your heart.

The gift for making music does not appear in any of the lists of spiritual gifts. Why do you suppose it is not included? What other gifts that greatly enrich the church do not appear in the lists of spiritual gifts?

1 Samuel 16:16-17, 22

"Let our LORD now command the servants who attend you to look for someone who is skillful in playing the lyre; and when the evil spirit from God is upon you, he will play it, and you will feel better." So Saul said to his servants, "Provide for me someone who can play well, and bring him to me." . . . Saul sent to Jesse, saying, "Let David remain in my service, for he has found favor in my sight."

Note: What do you want to remember from this week's meeting? What passions, gifts, and talents did you notice in group members?

Beyond the Lists of "Ordinary" **GIFTS**

SESSION FOUR

Till All Come to *Maturity*

SESSION FOUR

Day 1 **

Read Galatians 1:13-18. Read again Galatians 1:13-18.

We tend to think that after his conversion, Saul/Paul immediately became a missionary and writer of what would later be much of the New Testament. But here Paul tells us otherwise. After his conversion, he retreated into the desert and stayed there three years. Then he learned from other leaders in the church, and finally he began his public ministry.

[ENTRY POINT: **Off to Desert U.**]

How and from whom have you learned about the faith? Do you have someone you consider a "spiritual father" or "spiritual mother," or a special friend who has made a significant difference in your journey? How have these people helped you learn about yourself? What and how have you learned directly from God?

As you look back on your growth in faith, what time would you consider your spiritual infancy? Today, are you a teenager, a young adult, a "middler," or a senior adult in your faith?

Where is your growing edge right now in using your gifts and talents to serve God?

Galatians 1:13-18

You have heard, no doubt, of my earlier life in Judaism. I was violently persecuting the church of God and was trying to destroy it. I advanced in Judaism beyond many among my people of the same age, for I was far more zealous for the traditions of my ancestors. But when God, who had set me apart before I was born and called me through his grace, was pleased to reveal his Son to me, so that I might proclaim him among the Gentiles, I did not confer with any human being, nor did I go up to Jerusalem to those who were already apostles before me, but I went away at once into Arabia, and afterwards I returned to Damascus. Then after three years I did go up to Jerusalem to visit Cephas and stayed with him fifteen days.

SESSION FOUR — *Day 2*

Read Matthew 25:14-28. Read again Matthew 25:20-21.

Think about two people you know well. In your mind or on this page, list "talents" you see God has entrusted to each person. Don't forget abilities like helping people (and the means by which they do that), organizing, managing money well, and so on.

[ENTRY POINT: **Use 'em or Lose 'em?**]

Now make a similar list of the talents God has entrusted to you. As you reflect on these lists of gifts, are you reminded of one of the servants in this parable? Who has been given five talents, two, one? How well has each person invested his or her talents? What keeps them—or you—from using these God-given talents?

Consider what creative activity or ability God may be calling you to develop or to try again, particularly one that is just for fun. List some activities that re-create you. How do you cooperate with God's desire to renew you?

Matthew 25:20-21

Then the one who had received the five talents came forward, bringing five more talents, saying, "Master, you handed over to me five talents; see, I have made five more talents." His master said to him, "Well done, good and trustworthy slave; you have been trustworthy in a few things, I will put you in charge of many things; enter into the joy of your master."

SESSION FOUR — *Day 3*

Read Psalm 40:1-3. Read again Psalm 40:1-3.

The psalmist traces a process of God's work of rescue and deliverance: being taken from a horrible pit, to clay, to solid ground, to being able to sing.

[**ENTRY POINT:** **New Eyes to See, New Ears to Hear**]

Thinking back over the last several years, how have you seen God work gradually in your life?

If you were to write your own "new song" about God's activity in your life, what three or four events would you include? Now actually write a few sentences and sing them as an act of thanks for what God has done for you. Make up your own tune or sing your words to a familiar tune that seems appropriate.

In addition to seeing God's work, in later verses this psalmist also gives thanks for an open ear to hear God. We see God's work or hear God's voice because God gives us the ability to do so. But we can also act to improve our attention to God. What practices or experiences have helped you to see God and to listen more attentively for God's guidance? How has God opened your eyes and ears?

Psalm 40:1-3

I waited patiently for the Lord;
  he inclined to me and heard my cry.

He drew me up from the desolate pit,
  out of the miry bog,
and set my feet upon a rock, making my steps
  secure.

He put a new song in my mouth,
  a song of praise to our God.
Many will see and fear,
  and put their trust in the Lord.

SESSION FOUR

Read Deuteronomy 31:1-8, 14-15, 23. Read again Deuteronomy 31:14.

Moses is given an opportunity that many of us will not have—he knows that his death is at hand.

[**ENTRY POINT:** **Last Words**]

If God were to tell you that you had just one year left to live, how would you spend it? What relationships would you need to address? On what form of ministry would you focus? How would you reprioritize your life? Whom would you want to train or to whom would you want to give special instructions before you died?

How do you want your tombstone to read? Draw it in the space below and fill in the text you want to appear on it. Consider what you need to do now in order to make those words true.

Deuteronomy 31:14
The LORD said to Moses, "Your time to die is near; call Joshua and present yourselves in the tent of meeting, so that I may commission him." So Moses and Joshua went and presented themselves in the tent of meeting.

SESSION FOUR — Day 5

Read 2 Corinthians 9:6-15. Read again 2 Corinthians 9:11-15.

John Chrysostom wrote in *On the Letter to the Romans*: "If you give gladly, even if you give only a little, it is a big gift. If you give unwillingly, even if you give a big gift, you turn it into a small one." When have you given willingly? When have you given grudgingly? How has your giving changed over time?

[ENTRY POINT: **Sowing Generously**]

What is the best gift you have ever received? What is the best gift you have ever given?

In what ways are you "rich"? What has God given you that you use to enrich God's people? to enrich the poor?

2 Corinthians 9:11-15

You will be enriched in every way for your great generosity, which will produce thanksgiving to God through us; for the rendering of this ministry not only supplies the needs of the saints but also overflows with many thanksgivings to God. Through the testing of this ministry you glorify God by your obedience to the confession of the gospel of Christ and by the generosity of your sharing with them and with all others, while they long for you and pray for you because of the surpassing grace of God that he has given you. Thanks be to God for his indescribable gift!

Note: What do you want to remember from this week's meeting? What passions, gifts, and talents did you notice in group members?

SESSION FIVE

With a Little Help from

My Friends

SESSION FIVE

Day 1 **

Read Luke 1:41-56. Read again Luke 1:41-42.

"What happiness, what security, what joy to have someone to whom you dare to speak on terms of equality as to another self," wrote the twelfth-century monk Aelred of Rievaulx in *Spiritual Friendship*.* What an apt description of Mary and Elizabeth's spiritual kinship as both women face unusual yet joyous circumstances!

[ENTRY POINT: **Courage to Leap**]

Recall some of the special friendships you've experienced during your lifetime. Who have been the Elizabeths in your life? Who has encouraged you as you tried something new or helped you to "leap" in faith when you were on the brink of responding to God? How did that person or those persons nurture, support, or prod you?

Write a note or an e-mail message to one of your Elizabeths—a few sentences saying thanks for helping you grow or for encouraging you. Call an old friend to reminisce, and schedule time to visit or share a meal as soon as possible.

For whom have you been an Elizabeth in the past? For whom are you an encourager and friend in faith right now? Give thanks for the opportunity to be in relationships of trust and mutual faith. Pray for those yearning or searching for a Christian friend right now.

Luke 1:41-42

When Elizabeth heard Mary's greeting, the child leaped in her womb. And Elizabeth was filled with the Holy Spirit and exclaimed with a loud cry, "Blessed are you among women, and blessed is the fruit of your womb."

* Notre Dame, IN: Ave Maria Press, 2008, 59.

SESSION FIVE

Read 1 Kings 19:19-21. Read again 1 Kings 19:19-21.

The mantle was the prophet's most important article of clothing.

An animal skin or woolen cloak, it served as a coat, a blanket, a satchel to carry goods, and a bundle to sit on, as well as security for a debt. A prophet's mantle identified one who spoke for God.

[ENTRY POINT: **Passing the Mantle**]

Search your photo album, apartment or house, garage, attic. What are the most important things you own? What possessions, perhaps those that have been passed down through generations, are rich with meaning? What items convey your family's heritage and spiritual identity? Gather these objects together and decide how to preserve them. How do they tell the story of your life or the story of your family and heritage?

1 Kings 19:19-21

So he set out from there, and found Elisha son of Shaphat, who was plowing. There were twelve yoke of oxen ahead of him, and he was with the twelfth. Elijah passed by him and threw his mantle over him. He left the oxen, ran after Elijah, and said, "Let me kiss my father and my mother, and then I will follow you." Then Elijah said to him, "Go back again; for what have I done to you?" He returned from following him, took the yoke of oxen, and slaughtered them; using the equipment from the oxen, he boiled their flesh, and gave it to the people, and they ate. Then he set out and followed Elijah, and became his servant.

SESSION FIVE — *Day 3*

Read Acts 8:26-38. Read again Acts 8:29-38.

Evangelism means telling the good news of Christ

and preparing the way for people to come to belief, but we tend to think of evangelism and evangelists as showy and public. However, Philip's quiet conversation with the eunuch offers a picture of gentle, private evangelism. Have you conversed in this way about your faith? Do you consider such conversations evangelism?

[ENTRY POINT: **Quiet Evangelism**]

Think of someone you know who you believe has the spiritual gift of evangelism. What characteristics accompany this gift, in your mind? Do you have the gift of evangelism? If so, how do you know that? If not, why would you like to have it or not like to have it?

Acts 8:29-38

Then the Spirit said to Philip, "Go over to this chariot and join it." So Philip ran up to it and heard [the eunuch] reading the prophet Isaiah. He asked, "Do you understand what you are reading?" He replied, "How can I, unless someone guides me?" And he invited Philip to get in and sit beside him. Now the passage of the scripture that he was reading was this: "Like a sheep he was led to the slaughter, and like a lamb silent before its shearer, so he does not open his mouth. In his humiliation justice was denied him. Who can describe his generation? For his life is taken away from the earth." The eunuch asked Philip, "About whom, may I ask you, does the prophet say this, about himself or about someone else?" Then Philip began to speak, and starting with this scripture, he proclaimed to him the good news about Jesus. As they were going along the road, they came to some water; and the eunuch said, "Look, here is water! What is to prevent me from being baptized?" He commanded the chariot to stop, and both of them, Philip and the eunuch, went down into the water, and Philip baptized him.

SESSION FIVE

Read Exodus 6:28–7:2. Read again Exodus 6:28–7:2.

Reading this story, we might say either that Moses knew his limits and was wise or that he was simply making excuses.

Recall an occasion when you were challenged to do something for the first time. What did you feel as you considered the request or order? When have you considered a request and said no because you knew your own limits? When have you simply made excuses? In general, how do people respond when someone says no?

[ENTRY POINT: **Excuses or Self-Knowledge?**]

For what reasons should we say no to requests to engage in ministry?

Exodus 6:28–7:2

On the day when the Lord spoke to Moses in the land of Egypt, he said to him, "I am the Lord; tell Pharaoh king of Egypt all that I am speaking to you." But Moses said in the Lord's presence, "Since I am a poor speaker, why would Pharaoh listen to me?"

The Lord said to Moses, "See, I have made you like God to Pharaoh, and your brother Aaron shall be your prophet. You shall speak all that I command you, and your brother Aaron shall tell Pharaoh to let the Israelites go out of his land."

SESSION FIVE

Read 1 Samuel 3:1-10. Read again 1 Samuel 3:8-10.

The old priest Eli is blind. The inexperienced boy Samuel serves in the Temple, even sleeping there at night. But when God speaks to Samuel, Samuel does not recognize the voice waking him as God's voice. Three times Samuel goes to Eli. Eli realizes that God is speaking to the boy, and he tells Samuel how to respond in a way that welcomes God. Like Samuel, we all have to learn to recognize God's voice.

[ENTRY POINT: **Those Who Help Us Listen**]

Often we need the counsel of others to help us pay attention to God. Reflect on your spiritual journey and consider the Eli figures in your life. With whom have you talked about God? Who has instructed you about welcoming God more fully? What advice has helped you?

Samuel was deep inside organized religion, yet he had trouble hearing God. Is it sometimes harder for God to get through to "insiders"—those deeply involved in the church? What might make this so? What can insiders do to be sure we continue to listen to God?

How could you be an Eli to someone newer to faith than you are?

1 Samuel 3:8-10

The Lord called Samuel again, a third time. And he got up and went to Eli, and said, "Here I am, for you called me." Then Eli perceived that the Lord was calling the boy. Therefore Eli said to Samuel, "Go, lie down; and if he calls you, you shall say, 'Speak, Lord, for your servant is listening.'" So Samuel went and lay down in his place. Now the Lord came and stood there, calling as before, "Samuel! Samuel!" And Samuel said, "Speak, for your servant is listening."

Note: What do you want to remember from this week's meeting? What passions, gifts, and talents did you notice in group members?

SESSION SIX

Not Hearers *Only*

SESSION SIX

Read Romans 11:25-29. Read again Romans 11:29.

The gifts and the calling of God are "irrevocable."

What comes to mind when you hear the word *irrevocable*? What feelings do you associate with something being irrevocable? How do you feel when you consider that the gifts God has given you will never be taken away?

[**ENTRY POINT: Gifts That Keep on Giving**]

Draw the outline of a large gift box. Within it, write words that describe several things you can do well. Do you consider these gifts from God? Regardless of your answer, how could and how do you use them to serve God?

Draw another, smaller box. Within it, write words that describe some activities you used to do well but no longer engage in. Why did you stop doing them? Since God's gifts are never taken back, where are these gifts/aptitudes/talents being "stored"?

God's call to you, God's claim on you, will never wane, never be taken back. Sit in silence and pay attention to what you feel as you consider that amazing truth. What do you want to say to God in response?

Romans 11:29

. . . for the gifts and the calling of God are irrevocable.

SESSION SIX

Read Jonah 1:1-3; 4:10-11. Read again Jonah 1:1-3.

Jonah and his people have a keen awareness of their relationship with God. Error creeps in when Jonah begins to consider God his exclusive possession.

[**ENTRY POINT:** **God of All?**]

Jonah would rather flee from God than give up his narrow views about who deserves to know God and experience God's mercy.

Think about those whom you consider impervious to change. Are you tempted to steer clear of them? Are you trying to ignore God's clear leading to become involved? How can you let Jonah's negative example remind you that God is not willing that anyone should perish (2 Pet. 3:9)? In prayer, name two or three people desperately in need of God's gracious intervention.

Jonah 1:1-3

Now the word of the LORD came to Jonah son of Amittai, saying, "Go at once to Nineveh, that great city, and cry out against it; for their wickedness has come up before me." But Jonah set out to flee to Tarshish from the presence of the LORD. He went down to Joppa and found a ship going to Tarshish; so he paid his fare and went on board, to go with them to Tarshish, away from the presence of the LORD.

Handwritten note:

2 PETER 3:9

THE LORD IS NOT SLACK CONCERNING HIS PROMISE AS SOME COUNT SLACKNESS BUT IS LONGSUFFERING TOWARD US NOT WILLING THAT ANY SHOULD PERISH BUT THAT ALL SHOULD COME TO REPENTANCE

SESSION SIX

Read Exodus 3:1-12. Read again Exodus 3:11-12.

The burning bush can be seen as a metaphor for all of creation—it is afire with God.

This story illustrates that any place can become a meeting place with God and that God can break into our lives when we least expect it. Who would have thought that simply going to work in the morning (as Moses did) could lead to an experience that would turn one's whole life around? When we encounter God, we become more profoundly aware of the Presence that is around us, within us, and yet beyond us.

[ENTRY POINT: **Burning Bushes**]

Have you ever had a "burning bush" experience?

Recall a person or event that gave you a special sense of encounter with the Holy One. How has that experience changed your life? Form the habit of imagining the people you see on the street, the trees in the neighborhood, the place where you spend most of your day, ablaze with fire. What you see with your soul may be truer than what you see with your physical eyes.

Exodus 3:11-12

But Moses said to God, "Who am I that I should go to Pharaoh, and bring the Israelites out of Egypt?" He said, "I will be with you; and this shall be the sign for you that it is I who sent you: when you have brought the people out of Egypt, you shall worship God on this mountain."

SESSION SIX — *Day 4*

Read Acts 11:20-26. Read again Acts 11:22-24.

Barnabas's name means "son of encouragement." Take a moment to make a list of words you think your family members and coworkers might use to describe you. Then look at your list, sit in silence, and envision the picture created by it. Consider what your "name" might be. Are you a "son of mercy"? a "daughter of faith"? What would you say is your identity?

[ENTRY POINT: **Children of Encouragement**]

What would you like your name or identity to be as a person of faith? Sit in silence, holding that image in your mind as a prayer. Ask God to open your eyes to opportunities to become this person, and to give you courage to live in ways that reflect the best of what God wants you to be. What step could you take this week toward becoming this person?

Acts 11:22-24

News of this came to the ears of the church in Jerusalem, and they sent Barnabas to Antioch. When he came and saw the grace of God, he rejoiced, and he exhorted them all to remain faithful to the Lord with steadfast devotion; for he was a good man, full of the Holy Spirit and of faith. And a great many people were brought to the Lord.

SESSION SIX

Read Isaiah 50:4-5. Read again Isaiah 50:4-5.

In verse 4 the prophet identifies a gift God has given him ("the tongue of a teacher"), what he is to do with it ("sustain"), with whom ("the weary"), and by what means ("a word"). It reads almost like a personal mission statement. Using Isaiah's model, consider what God has given you—perhaps the heart of a nurturer or the hands of a healer or builder, the mind of a scientist, the passion of an artist, the wisdom and patience of a teacher. If you were asked to come up with one word or phrase to describe yourself, what would it be?

[ENTRY POINT: **Who, What, Where, How**]

How do you think God wants you to use your gift? Are you meant to help others, to teach, to lead, to entertain, to inspire? What do you truly love to do?

Isaiah was called to help "the weary." To what group or endeavor has God called you? Is there a group of people whom you have always cared about—children, the aged, teenagers, those with special needs, those who are ill, the homeless and marginalized, the hungry? To whom do you feel drawn?

By what means are you called to serve and support others? (To give you some ideas: organizing, raising money, working within the political system to change laws; being a writer, an artist, a teacher, an administrator; working behind the scenes as a helper, or directly serving people in need.)

Isaiah 50:4-5

The Lord God has given me the tongue of a teacher, that I may know how to sustain the weary with a word. Morning by morning he wakens—wakens my ear to listen as those who are taught. The Lord God has opened my ear, and I was not rebellious, I did not turn backward.

Meeting God in
Service

TEN CHAIRS WERE PULLED close together in a circle, but we were all leaning forward to catch Mary Jean's words. She seldom spoke during our small-group meetings, yet this week she seemed eager to talk. She described the time she had spent working in a community center and the relentless problems of poverty, addiction, and abuse she had encountered there. Tears came to her eyes as she concluded, "I feel helpless as I look at these families and see their suffering. What does God expect of me? How can I make a difference?"

Like Mary Jean, we may struggle to see just how God acts in a world of great suffering. And when it comes to our own role, we often don't know where to begin or what God might be asking of us. We sometimes feel overwhelmed, or we want to turn away from the realities that surround us. Yet as we begin to serve others, we often find our hesitations fading. We discover that when we help others, we encounter God. We meet God in the midst of our efforts. This can happen in several ways.

LEARNING TO LOOK

We learn to see God by opening our eyes and actively looking for opportunities to serve others. From the beginning of his ministry, Jesus constantly stayed alert to people and their needs. It was one reason why he came. Jesus read from the book of Isaiah in the synagogue at Nazareth, applying these words to himself:

"The Spirit of the Lord is upon me,
because he has anointed me
to bring good news to the poor.
He has sent me to proclaim release to the captives
and recovery of sight to the blind,
to let the oppressed go free,
to proclaim the year of the Lord's favor."—Luke 4:18-19

Every day as he traveled with his disciples, Jesus healed and fed and loved people. A number of stories in the Gospels tell us that Jesus acted because he was moved with compassion. As painful as it must have been sometimes, he did not turn aside from seeing people suffer.

Jesus not only saw the sufferings of human beings but also became involved in people's suffering to heal and bring new life. The story of the widow of Nain in Luke 7:11-17 illustrates this. As Jesus travels with his disciples and a crowd of followers, he encounters a funeral procession. The widow, he discovers, has lost her only son. Jesus sees her grief with eyes of compassion, knowing that as a widow she has been completely dependent on her son. Now she has no one—and nothing. Jesus says to her, "Do not weep," and raises the young man back to life. Then we find the words, "Jesus gave him to his mother" (v. 15). What compassion and mercy are captured in those words!

Again and again Jesus actively seeks the sick and needy. He goes directly to them; he notices their pain and suffering and responds with divine grace and love. The common activities of his life—travels, conversations, seemingly chance meetings with people—become the settings for expressions of his caring alertness. He appropriately perceives himself as a servant of God, and in serving God he ministers to those God loves.

LEARNING TO LISTEN

In the Gospel of John, Jesus demonstrates that this open-eyed attitude of caring was not to be confined only to his own ministry but was to characterize the lives of his followers as well. Jesus washed the disciples' feet as they gathered to celebrate the festival of the Passover, in part to remind us of our proper posture before others: "You call me Teacher and Lord—and you are right, for that is what I am. So if I, your Lord and Teacher, have washed your feet, you also ought to wash one another's feet" (John 13:13-14). Not only do we open our eyes to need; we also listen to those we serve. We cannot know how to help others if we simply barge in to "fix" a list of problems we think we see in them. We must serve others with gentle openness to them and with a willingness to relinquish our own agenda. We listen to their ideas and hopes and longings.

To listen requires a quieting of our own interests and experiences so that we can become open not only in that particular relationship but also to the ways in which God is present in the relationship. Henri J. M. Nouwen comments: "Real training for service asks for a hard and often painful process of self-emptying. The main problem of service is to be the way without being 'in the way'" (from *Reaching Out: The Three Movements of the Spiritual Life*).

Learning to become more open to others teaches us many things. Openness cultivates in us an attitude of honesty. We see ourselves as well as others more clearly. Then we are able to open ourselves to God—to name and surrender those parts of us that are wounded and in need of healing and forgiveness. Just as we speak of God's love for and forgiveness of others, so we can claim that healing in our own lives.

Our lives may be deeply changed as we serve others. As those we serve talk about their own pilgrimages, we see how God has been a part of their experiences. Their vision of God may enlarge ours. Their words, feelings, and desires may challenge us in surprising ways. When twentieth-century spiritual writer Evelyn Underhill went to Baron von Hügel for guidance about her relationship with God, he recommended that she spend a designated amount of time each week directly serving the poor so as to break open her heart to the needs of people and open her up more fully to experience God's grace. As a result, she met a woman named Laura Rose, the beginning of a relationship that was to become deeply significant for Underhill's spiritual growth.

LEARNING TO LOVE

To looking and listening we add loving—of the most radical, sacrificial kind. It is easy to be captured by our own special interests and by self-absorption. When we follow Jesus, however, normal priorities get turned upside down. We confront what German pastor and theologian Dietrich Bonhoeffer called "the cost of discipleship." God transforms our self-interest into a new awareness of our interdependence.

We identify the ways in which we need one another in order to grow in faithfulness. We find a new identity by centering our lives in the One who is the light of the world and who calls us to let our lights "shine before others, so that they may see [our] good works and give glory to [our] Father in heaven" (Matt. 5:16). We realize that nothing matters more than bringing people to Christ for healing and salvation.

Little by little our hearts, which can so easily become hardened to the needs of others, are changed into caring and compassionate hearts. Thomas Kelly, in his book *A Testament of Devotion*, captures this phenomenon in these words: "God plucks the world out of our hearts, loosening the chains of attachment. And He hurls the world into our hearts, where we and He together carry it in infinitely tender love."

<u>RESOURCES TO GET US THROUGH</u>

The radical call to service does not pose for us an impossible duty, however. God promises to give us the power and resources we need through the indwelling Spirit of Christ. Paul wrote to the new converts in the first-century church in Corinth to remind them of their calling. Paul pointed out that he had come to them in weakness, fear, and trembling but that God had used him to demonstrate the power of the Spirit (see 1 Cor. 1:18-31; 2:6-13). What freedom there is in knowing that God can use us in spite of our weaknesses!

Indeed, power is released through our vulnerability. It is through our vulnerabilities that we learn the nature of God's sufficiency. The only way we can confront head-on the pain of a suffering world is through utter reliance on God's grace. We can take to heart God's word to Paul, "My grace is sufficient for you, for power is made perfect in weakness" (2 Cor. 12:9).

Christ is inviting us to love the world as he loves. Paul encouraged a congregation of Christians who were undergoing much struggle by reminding them that they were a letter of Christ, written not with ink but with the Spirit of the living God (2 Cor. 3:2-3). What a word of promise for today! We go in the power of the Spirit, and the Spirit speaks in and through what we do.

"Christian ministry," writes James Fenhagen in *Ministry and Solitude*, "is more than doing good. Ministry is an act of service performed either consciously or unconsciously in the name of Christ. Ministry is Jesus Christ expressing his life through us." When we are tempted to run and hide because the needs of the world are overwhelming and we feel helpless to make a difference, we can remember that we do not go alone. We venture out boldly, not because we underestimate or devalue the needs and woundedness of others but because we trust in the steadfast and abiding love of God.

In serving the needs of others in society, we meet God. We find joy, as Brother Lawrence found centuries ago, "doing little things for the love of God." And as we grow, we learn more about the love of Christ and what it means to share it with others. This prayer in Ephesians describes what it means to mature in our relationship with Christ: "I pray that, according to the riches of his glory, he may grant that you may be strengthened in your inner being with power through his Spirit, and that Christ may dwell in your hearts through faith, as you are being rooted and grounded in love" (Eph. 3:16-17).

Meeting God in *Community*

WE WERE NOT created to live in isolation. No person "is an island, entire of itself," wrote the poet John Donne. While no one questions the need for periods of solitude and refreshment in our lives, faith tends to thrive most readily when shared and experienced with others. Without the connections community affords us, we experience what someone once called "spiritual loneliness." For we meet God not just as we sit alone in quiet corners but in and through the people with whom we live, work, and interact as we go through our daily routine.

Relationships present us with both a remarkable privilege and an awesome responsibility. Proverbs 27:17 tells us that "iron sharpens iron, and one person sharpens [and shapes] . . . another." As other people's lives touch ours, they help to form our faith and make us who we are. As we touch others, we reflect God's love to them. Relationships with other believers have extraordinary power in our lives because Christ is present in them. Jesus knew how important people are in conveying God's grace and presence. "Where two or three are gathered in my name," he said, "I am there among them" (Matt. 18:20). Within our churches, small groups, families, and friendships, we learn from one another. We find encouragement. We challenge one another to follow God more faithfully. Other Christians enable us to walk as we should when we might otherwise have strayed or wandered. God uses relationships to form us, and relationships form us so that God can use us.

POWER FOR GROWTH AND CHANGE

The Bible offers many examples of the formational power of relationships. The story of Ruth and Naomi demonstrates how the presence of other believers can enable us to do what we can't do alone. Ruth is a foreigner, a "Moabitess" who has married Naomi's son. When Naomi's husband and her sons (including Ruth's husband) die, she grieves, saying, "The hand of the Lord has turned against me" (Ruth 1:13). Ruth, also widowed, chooses to stay with Naomi rather than return to her own kin. Ruth speaks the words that are well-known and much-loved: "Where you go, I will go; where you lodge, I will lodge; your people shall be my people, and your God my God" (Ruth 1:16). Just think of the magnitude of the change those words brought about! Something in this relationship makes Ruth willing to leave her family and country to adopt Naomi's faith. The younger woman seeks guidance from Naomi and in turn cares for her. Through their loving relationship Naomi is released from the bitterness of her losses, and Ruth is drawn into relationship with the God of Israel. Eventually Ruth becomes an ancestor of Jesus the Messiah (see Matt. 1:5).

Elijah and Elisha offer an example of the way God uses the power of relationships to build strong leaders. Employing Elijah as Elisha's mentor, God makes a dramatic difference in the life of the younger man who is eager to serve God faithfully. Elijah, a famous prophet, is near the end of his ministry when God tells him to seek out and anoint Elisha as his successor. Elijah throws his cloak over Elisha's shoulders as the younger man walks behind his plow and his oxen, publicly calling Elisha to a new way of life. What a dramatic act! Elisha leaves his farm work to become Elijah's attendant (see 1 Kings 19:16-21), following the prophet and seeking to learn from him. He refuses to leave his mentor and asks for "a double share" of the spirit that has made Elijah great (see 2 Kings 2:9). One man is clearly the teacher and the other the student; and, like Elijah, Elisha acknowledges that God is at the center of his life and ministry. Through his relationship with Elijah, he develops the courage, faith, and skills to carry on the work of the prophet as God's spokesperson.

In the New Testament, Mary and Elizabeth offer us yet another example of how relationships help us mature in faith. Their relationship illustrates the value of sharing mutual insight and encouragement. According to the Gospel of Luke, young Mary is visited by the angel Gabriel, who tells her that she will bear a son who will be the Messiah. Mary, "much perplexed by his words" (Luke 1:29), hurries to visit her older cousin Elizabeth, who is also pregnant. Though Mary has told the angel that she wants to be obedient to God's will, she is surely also confused and frightened. But after Elizabeth speaks to her, Mary breaks into a song of praise to God; her faith has been strengthened. Mary spends three months with Elizabeth, who supports her and in turn is supported in the joyful yet sacrificial work to which God has called both of them. Mary discovered, as many have, that when we are hesitant to face what lies ahead, spending time with someone who knows us and shares our faith can help us see more clearly and understand more deeply the issues we need to deal with. It fortifies us to move forward in faith.

SOUL FRIENDS

Throughout the history of the church, writers and leaders have echoed this message. In the twelfth century, Aelred of Rievaulx asserted that Christian friendship can be "a step to raise us to the love and knowledge of God." He spoke about the joy of having a friend with "whom you need have no fear to confess your failings; one to whom you can unblushingly make known what progress you have made in the spiritual life; one to whom you can entrust all the secrets of your heart and before whom you can place all your plans" (from "On Spiritual Friendship," translated by Mary Eugenia Laker). Teresa of Avila wrote in the sixteenth century: "It is a great advantage for us to be able to consult someone who knows us, so that we may learn to know ourselves." John Wesley went so far as to declare there is no such thing as a solitary Christian.

What these Christians from various times and places learned is that God uses close and continuing relationships to form us in the image of Christ. As we share both our high moments and our low, pray for one another, help each other, and work together toward common goals, we reflect Christ and acknowledge God's presence with us.

NURTURING YOUR OWN SOUL FRIENDS

To begin to meet God in community, you may want to reach out to other believers with whom you can discuss your spiritual journey. Such conversation helps you to sort out what you know about yourself and about God. It may be especially valuable if you make this a deliberate action. Ask one or two mature individuals—with whom you can exchange thoughts and prayers with confidence and assurance of confidentiality—to meet with you. This practice has traditionally been called "spiritual guidance," "spiritual direction," or "spiritual friendship."

This kind of conversation may also occur in the context of worship services, church-school classes, and small groups. One-on-one relationships and small groups allow for a depth of interaction not possible in larger, more formal settings. They allow us to pray aloud for one another with potentially life-changing results. As Alan Jones, an essayist on Christian friendship, stated, "We cannot help but tremble on the brink of surrender, but it is our companions who give us the courage to jump" (from "Exploring Spiritual Direction: An Essay on Christian Friendship").

SPEND TIME OBSERVING THE LIVES OF FAITHFUL CHRISTIANS

The New Testament tells us repeatedly that we become like Christ by spending time with those who are Christ's friends. We look at those who have led us, consider the outcome of their faith, and then choose to imitate them (see Heb. 13:7). Some find it a good discipline to think periodically about someone whose faith they admire. Consider approaching one or more such people to ask them how God has been at work in their lives. (For biblical examples of this process, see 1 Cor. 4:6; Phil. 3:17; 1 Thess. 1:6; and 2 Thess. 3:9.)

STAY ACTIVE IN A CHURCH COMMUNITY

As happens within our immediate family circle, when we rub shoulders with others, we are continually confronted with reminders of our weaknesses and brokenness. We wound others and are wounded by them. Romans 12:18 acknowledges that living with others can be difficult, urging, "If it is possible, so far as it depends on you, live peaceably with all."

While imperfections abound within what Paul calls "the body of Christ," God still uses the company of believers to grace our lives and transform the world (see Rom. 12:4-5; 1 Cor. 12:12; Eph. 5:30). We cannot do without our fellow believers. The writer of the letter to the Hebrews urges Christians not to neglect to meet together (Heb. 10:25). At their best, relationships with other believers not only shield us in difficult times but also help us to confront our imperfections. We find a place to mutually speak "the truth in love" (Eph. 4:15).

VIEW YOUR INVOLVEMENT WITH OTHER BELIEVERS AS AN OPPORTUNITY TO HELP

It is a privilege to nurture another person, to be trusted to hear another's dreams and concerns, to pray for someone. In so doing we may discover myriad ways to use the gifts that God has given us, to benefit our family in Christ as well as for our own growth and enjoyment. As we help others, we too will be helped. As we comfort and teach and encourage, we will be comforted, taught, and encouraged in turn. As we experience community, we find our lives enriched, in turn providing us with more to give to others.

Meeting God in *Everyday Life*

"WE LIVE LIVES OF LITTLE THINGS," someone once said. We are occupied most often with the details of ordinary life. Driving to the office or factory, putting supper on the table, taking feverish kids to the doctor—these are the things that fill our hours. When we meet God, that encounter often takes place in and through everyday circumstances. Growing spiritually will mean "living to God on common occasions," as Horace Bushnell expressed it. Inevitably we cultivate our spiritual lives not just in quiet solitude but in the activity of everyday life. We realize that God speaks to us not just in sky-rending revelations but also in the intimacy of quiet conversation with someone we love, the freshness of a child's spontaneous observation, the warmth of a bubbling pot of chili, the comfort of a familiar household ritual.

How do we meet God in the midst of our stressful, busy lives? How do we recognize the signs that, in Avery Brooke's wonderful phrase, lie "hidden in plain sight"?

Two intentions will help us:

REMEMBER GOD'S DEEDS

The Bible leaves no doubt that God works through the inner and outer details of our everyday lives. And if God is present in such moments, we cannot let them slide into oblivion: "Watch yourselves closely, so as neither to forget the things that your eyes have seen nor to let them slip from your mind all the days of your life" (Deut. 4:9). The psalmist, recalling God's careful involvement in Israel's history, vowed, "I will call to mind the deeds of the Lord; I will remember your wonders of old" (Ps. 77:11).

The act of remembering helped the people of Israel to keep events from the past vital in the present. Just as we pull out a photo album on a rainy day in order to recall the significant moments of our lives—to review the snapshots of graduations and baptisms, visits and vacations—so God wanted the people of Israel to keep their holy history vividly present in their minds. And they were to remember God's good deeds corporately, as a people. Recollection was a community event. As they gathered in various ways, the people recalled aloud the moments that had given them identity as people of God—when God led them to freedom from Egyptian bondage, gave them commandments and instruction, gave them life. "Remember the former things of old," Isaiah enjoined the people, speaking on God's behalf (Isa. 46:9). The Israelites' very identity depended on the God who had acted in their history. To forget God's acts would have meant to forget that God had called and chosen them.

God's call to remember carried over into New Testament times. Jesus urged his followers to commemorate God's work of redemption. "Do this in remembrance of me," he said at the Last Supper (Luke 22:19). Communion, in which we partake of the bread and the cup, is a supreme act of remembering. We also meet God through recalling what he has done for us personally. With David the psalmist we make certain that we "do not forget all [God's] benefits" in our daily lives (Ps. 103:2). To jog his readers' memories, David recites specific benefits. He does not indulge in nostalgia but gleans from the past what the Lord did and said. When we remember the Lord's deeds, we likewise keep in the forefront of our minds what God has already shown us; we live in continuity with the events that have shaped us. We recall the blessings of last year and the hardships of last week, remembering how God walked beside us and sometimes carried us in our moments of weakness and woundedness.

Conscious recollection requires discipline. In a live-for-the-moment culture, we may find the act of remembering more difficult than ancient people did. We are prone to become distracted by the details of the moment. We forget to "read life backwards." But memory can be a powerful resource for keeping our spiritual perspective alive.

One practical aid to this holy remembering is keeping a journal. Many find it helpful to jot down prayers, record insights from Bible readings, or put on paper the events that seem to be leading somewhere—events that have left an impression on them. Keeping a journal can be done in a way that meets your own needs and preferences. Journaling need not be an elaborate affair or something you slavishly do every day. It can be as simple as you wish and as occasional as meets your need. If you have never used a journal, try taking a blank bound book, a spiral notebook, or a binder full of paper—and then simply write. Make your writing an act of sanctified listening. When you write down your thoughts and ideas and emotions, they take definition and shape. You may find that as you write, you begin to untangle your confusion about what you are hearing from God. You may hear God speaking in ways that you may not have been attentive to otherwise.

Do not allow yourself to relegate to a fuzzy memory the significant events and changes going on within and around you. "The simplest ink," says an old Chinese proverb, "is more reliable than the finest mind." Writing becomes a way to extract deeper meaning from what has happened to you. It becomes an act of remembering.

Leaf back through your journal pages every few weeks. Notice how God's purposes seem to be emerging in what has happened—and in what hasn't happened. Thank God for prayers that have been answered. Continue to lift up to God themes that emerge from what you've written, themes that reveal your heart's desires. And watch for a greater sense of personal direction. Keeping a journal, wrote Ronald Klug, is "like walking into a messy room—toys and clothes and books piled around—and slowly picking things up and putting them in their right places again. The room 'feels good' and I can go on living there. In a similar way, my journal helps me sort out things in my life and restore some internal order" (from *Keeping a Spiritual Journal*).

We can practice the art of remembering when we meet with family and friends. Conversations at family reunions might move beyond talk of sports or vacations to reflections about how God has proven faithful in our family's past and present stories. And when we go to church, worship can be an exercise in remembering. Spiritual-growth groups, church-school classes—any gathering of believers—can be an occasion to track God's actions. We recall ways God has been faithful. We "testify." When we do, we are reminded of who God is through what God has done.

REFLECT ON GOD'S DEEDS

Reflection—alert awareness of what is happening now—returns us to the present moment. Open-eyed reflection allows us to see God's hand at work or to grasp insights we might otherwise have been too busy to notice. The Bible sometimes uses the word *meditate* for this kind of thoughtful reflection. We are not talking about the meditation of Eastern religions nor a privatized, overly individualistic quest for religious experience. Biblical meditation is always God-centered. It often focuses on God's Word revealed in scripture. And it often has to do with God's activity. "On your wondrous works, I will meditate," David exults in Psalm 145:5. Just three verses earlier he had vowed, "Every day I will bless you." An awareness of what God is doing and the impulse to praise God go hand-in-hand.

Events of daily life therefore belong in our daily prayers. In the Lord's Prayer Jesus directs us to pray for God's will to be done on earth, not just in heaven—which means in our everyday lives. Knowing how much daily matters affect us, Jesus even encourages his followers to pray for "daily bread"—the everyday sustenance that keeps our physical bodies going. The likelihood that Jesus worked as a carpenter during his early adult years implies that God, through Jesus Christ's incarnation, has for all time graced daily work. And God notices when "bad" things happen and operates through events so that, as the apostle Paul wrote, "All things work together for good for those who love God" (Rom. 8:28). All the realities of life, then, constitute the grist for our conversations with God.

As we pray about what happens to us from moment to moment, we begin to cultivate spiritual alertness. Jean-Pierre de Caussade wrote of "the sacrament of the present moment." He meant that the place where we are, the actions that we take, can mediate God's presence. Writing of Mary and Joseph, Jesus' parents, de Caussade asks, "What do they discern beneath the seemingly everyday events which occupy them? What is seen is similar to what happens to the rest of [hu]mankind. But what is unseen, that which faith discovers and unravels, is nothing less than God fulfilling [a] mighty purpose. . . . God reveals [God]self to the humble in small things" (from *The Sacrament of the Present Moment,* translated by Kitty Muggeridge).

Reflection can take place in the workplace, where many of us spend much of our time. Martin Luther, one of the prime figures of the Protestant Reformation, argued that not just priest or nun but also milkmaid or blacksmith could become deeply conscious of God's presence. This awareness can happen in our busy times and during our leisure times. Thomas Kelly writes, "A life of little whispered words of adoration, of praise, of prayer, of worship can be breathed all through the day" (from *A Testament of Devotion*).

Staying alert to God's presence may be as simple as pausing to acknowledge that God is near. It may mean taking a few moments to pray during a lunch hour or coffee break. It may mean occasionally looking out the window to drink in the beauty of God's creation or paying care-filled attention to the people with whom we live. And it certainly means allowing everyday blessings—a sunset, a smile from a friend—to remind us of God and point us toward God in gratitude.

INTRODUCTION TO *Acts*

The Good News Spreads Under the Spirit's Guidance

This book might well be called "The Acts of the Holy Spirit." ***From beginning to end the Spirit guides the spread of the gospel from Jerusalem to Rome itself.*** Poured out on the day of Pentecost with "a sound like the rush of a violent wind" and "divided tongues, as of fire" (Acts 2:2-3), ***the Spirit changes lives, alters plans, and transforms situations.*** The Spirit empowers the early Christians to stand up to authorities, to face down mobs, to speak to hostile audiences, and to hold fast through suffering even to death—all for the sake of the good news of Jesus Christ. At the same time, the Spirit impels them far beyond their comfort zones into missions to the Samaritans and Gentiles and to people from all levels of society.

God's Spirit is active in our own lives—comforting, encouraging, strengthening, nudging. When have you felt led, like the early disciples, in a particular direction? When have you been the channel of God's love to someone else? When have you experienced a shower of grace when you needed it most? And when have you found resources of strength to do what seemed impossible? ***You have experienced the work of the Spirit***, sent by Jesus Christ who "is exalted at the right hand of God, and [who has] received from the Father the promise of the Holy Spirit, . . . [and] has poured out this that you both see and hear" (2:33).

> ***Key Verse:*** "But you will receive power when the Holy Spirit has come upon you; and you will be my witnesses in Jerusalem, in all Judea and Samaria, and to the ends of the earth."—Acts 1:8

INTRODUCTION TO *First Corinthians*

The Way of Love

In the apostle Paul's first letter to the Corinthians we encounter a missionary whose spirit is being transformed by the Holy Spirit. ***Paul urges the people of the Corinthian church to be likewise transformed by the Spirit of God.*** Paul admits that he is not a clever, eloquent orator but a childlike man who is "foolish" enough to preach the cross (1:17–2:16). ***His servant posture cuts through the barriers of human factions to pull together a community of believers*** who will proclaim in one voice that Jesus is Lord.

As you read Paul's letter and meditate on it, ***imagine yourself in the presence of the apostle, a seasoned spiritual teacher who crowns his letter with the often-quoted essay on love.*** Envision yourself telling Paul how hard it is for you to uphold this standard of love when you've had a spat with your spouse or felt misunderstood by your friend. Then turn your thoughts toward God in prayer. Ask God to help you cross the bridge between love in the abstract ("Of course I love people, but I can't stand my next-door neighbor!") and love in the concrete ("I know if I can learn to love my neighbor, then it won't be so hard to love other people"). ***How might such prayerful interaction with what Paul writes help you to become more loving—and part of a more loving community in Jesus Christ?***

> **Key Verses:** Love is patient; love is kind; love is not envious or boastful or arrogant or rude. It does not insist on its own way; it is not irritable or resentful; it does not rejoice in wrongdoing, but rejoices in the truth. It bears all things, believes all things, hopes all things, endures all things.
> —1 Corinthians 13:4-7

Introduction to Ephesians

Rooted in Love

This letter to the Ephesians reminds us of the importance of roots. The health of a tree is dependent on the health of its root system. Roots reach deep into the soil to draw up the necessary nourishment to sustain the tree. Deep roots create stability and help the tree withstand the storms of life. Likewise, *when we are rooted in the powerful and boundless love of Jesus, we are prepared to face the challenges of living in a stormy world.*

This letter calls us to imitate God (5:1) as the means of developing healthy roots. That task is made possible by being in a community of love with other Christians (4:12-16). Furthermore, *our life is energized by the unconditional grace of Jesus rather than by our own human efforts (2:4-10)*. Throughout this letter Paul (the attributed writer) offers prayers for his readers.

Pay attention to your own root system as you read and pray through Ephesians. *Pray that Jesus Christ will dwell within your heart more and more so that you are equipped to face the realities of life.* Consider the spiritual habits that have sustained you in the past. What new resources does this book offer to you? *How can you encourage others in the healthy planting of their roots deep into Jesus?*

> **Key Verses:** I pray . . . that Christ may dwell in your hearts through faith, as you are being rooted and grounded in love. I pray that you may have the power to comprehend, with all the saints, what is the breadth and length and height and depth, and to know the love of Christ that surpasses knowledge.—Ephesians 3:16-19

INTRODUCTION TO *Colossians*

A Heart Set on God

Sometimes we fool ourselves, believing it is more difficult to live today than two thousand years ago. However, the Christians of the first century faced equal or greater challenges to their faith. *The writer seeks to etch deeply into human hearts the truth that meaning and purpose do not come through any exclusive knowledge or superior spirituality.* Rather they are firmly established in the life of Jesus Christ, in whom God was pleased to dwell with all the divine fullness. Paul (the attributed writer) understands the serious crisis before his readers and seeks to weave these words into a fabric of practical guidance that clothes them with hearts that seek to focus on God. *In pondering these words of scripture, remember that the Bible uses the word* **heart** *to speak of mind, soul, and will.* How can the book of Colossians help you devote your life to God in all of these areas?

> **Key Verse:** So if you have been raised with Christ, seek the things that are above, where Christ is, seated at the right hand of God.—Colossians 3:1

Spiritual Gifts Inventory

Statements

1.	I am able to help people make choices and clarify decisions.
2.	I am aware of things without having to be told by anyone.
3.	I easily delegate authority and responsibility to others.
4.	I enjoy sharing my faith with the homeless and impoverished to offer hope.
5.	I enjoy teaching the Bible to a small group.
6.	I believe that God will help anyone in need.
7.	Through prayer, I see God's miraculous work in my life.
8.	I do not mind being made fun of for what I believe.
9.	I am able to organize human and material resources to serve the needs of others.
10.	I enjoy giving money to support the work of God.
11.	I like to work with people who are considered by others to be outcasts in their communities.
12.	Praying for the sick is a critical part of their healing.
13.	I can tell when Christian speakers or groups are being honest and faithful.
14.	I listen to others as carefully as I want them to listen to me.
15.	I would rather be a secretary in a group than the leader or chairperson.
16.	Whenever I share my faith, I ask others to share theirs as well.

17.	I help anyone in need, regardless of whether they deserve or appreciate the help.
18.	I am ready to counsel people who have spiritual, emotional, or physical problems.
19.	I can speak a foreign language fluently.
20.	I can follow the conversation of a foreign language I never studied.
21.	I am good at seeing many different sides to an issue and helping others see them as well.
22.	Things I understand by faith are confirmed by facts, experiences, or information.
23.	When I make a decision, I stand firmly behind it.
24.	I enjoy being part of ministries that didn't exist before.
25.	I am an effective mentor to other Christians.
26.	I see God at work in both good times and bad.
27.	I am aware of God's miracles every day.
28.	Others tell me I am a good public speaker.
29.	Working with others to minister to the physical needs of people is more enjoyable than doing the same thing by myself.
30.	I have enough money to give generously to important causes.
31.	I like to visit people wherever they are—at home, in the hospital, in prison, or in nursing homes.
32.	I believe that the healing power of God manifests itself in many different ways, not just in physical healing.
33.	I am able to identify the flaw in an argument, idea, or presentation.
34.	I learn best when I can discuss what I read in scripture and share insights and ideas with others.
35.	I am good at attending to the "busy work" that others tend not to enjoy.
36.	An invitation to Christian discipleship should be extended to people whenever they gather to worship or study.
37.	I give practical, material assistance to those who are in need.
38.	I will work hard to support any group that is fully committed to a good cause.
39.	Foreign languages are easy for me to learn.
40.	I intuitively understand the meanings of most foreign words and phrases.
41.	Others are surprised by the depth of my understanding and the integrity of my advice.
42.	I am good at sensing other people's moods and concerns just by being with them.
43.	I am effective at organizing projects for ministry.
44.	I desire the opportunity to be a missionary.

45.	I feel a strong responsibility to point out dangerous or erroneous teachings to others.
46.	I pray for people who have lost their faith.
47.	I believe that God works miracles through the faith of Christian believers.
48.	I find practical applications to real-world situations when I read the Bible.
49.	I find it easy to ask for help from others for worthy projects.
50.	I feel a strong desire to give money to Christian ministries.
51.	I want to help as many people as I can, regardless of the reason for their need.
52.	I pray for healing for the sick and afflicted.
53.	I know when a preacher or speaker is accurately presenting the gospel or spiritual teaching.
54.	It troubles me when people are misled or persuaded by inaccurate, biased, or false messages about the Christian faith.
55.	I give whatever time and energy is needed to finish a project or meet a deadline.
56.	I feel comfortable sharing the importance of Christian belief with non-Christians.
57.	I prefer working in the background rather than in the spotlight.
58.	I am patient and tolerant of others who are less mature in their spiritual development.
59.	I communicate easily with members of other races, cultures, or generations.
60.	I understand and easily accept the values, behaviors, and interests of generations other than my own.
61.	When others seek out my counsel or advice, I am confident that what I say will be helpful and valuable.
62.	People are surprised by how well I understand them.
63.	I offer good leadership to a project or group.
64.	It is easy for me to share my faith with people from other cultures and foreign lands.
65.	I strive to create harmony and unity whenever I am part of a group.
66.	I trust in the promises of God, even when they are improbable or unlikely.
67.	I feel the power and presence of God's Holy Spirit when I pray.
68.	My faith gives me the courage to speak out, even to those in positions of authority.
69.	I design and plan strategies for ministry both in and beyond the church.
70.	I know whether or not an appeal for money is legitimate.
71.	My compassion for others often takes precedence over my own personal needs.
72.	I participate in the healing of others through prayer.
73.	I intuitively sense elements of truth or error in other people's teachings.

74.	I enjoy creating lessons, classes, and projects that illuminate and illustrate biblical truths.
75.	Pastors and other key church leaders seek my opinions and advice on important issues.
76.	I feel comfortable talking about my faith in non-Christian settings.
77.	I make sure that everything runs as smoothly as possible.
78.	People are willing to listen to what I say because they understand that I have their best interests in mind.
79.	I communicate well with everyone, no matter how different from me they might be.
80.	I am able to interpret what someone says to others who do not understand.
81.	God grants me insights into the significant decisions that other people struggle with.
82.	My knowledge of the Bible and spiritual teachings provide me with answers to many of life's questions.
83.	I help others discover, develop, and use their spiritual gifts.
84.	I am proud to let people know I am a Christian everywhere I go.
85.	I like helping others apply Christian principles and practices to their daily lives.
86.	When I pray, my prayer becomes a channel for God's grace to meet other people's needs.
87.	God uses us as instruments of spiritual and supernatural power.
88.	I see how biblical truths apply as much to today's world as they did in their original context.
89.	Others refer to me as an effective leader.
90.	I seek the counsel of family, friends, or my spiritual community when I make a donation to charity or church.
91.	I listen to those who need someone to talk to.
92.	When I pray, I specifically name those who are in physical, spiritual, or emotional need.
93.	I know when a Christian leader is more "self-interested" than focused on God.
94.	I require evidence or proof before I accept something as valid or true.
95.	I am a better assistant than leader.
96.	The idea of sharing the gospel with others is very exciting to me.
97.	It is important to me that my actions make other people's lives easier or better.
98.	People go out of their way to please me.
99.	I can explain my spiritual practices to people of other cultures and backgrounds.
100.	I understand the meaning and significance of foreign rituals and practices, and can help interpret them for others.

101.	I know some things without fully understanding how I know them.
102.	I see potential problems that others are unaware of.
103.	I focus on the big picture instead of the details.
104.	I am comfortable with non-Christian lifestyles and customs.
105.	I look for ways to help others grow as Christian disciples.
106.	I spend long periods of time in prayer.
107.	I pray for things that other people feel are impossible.
108.	I enjoy showing people how the Bible relates to everyday life.
109.	I enjoy participating in ministries for the poor, needy, and marginalized.
110.	I am a cheerful giver of money.
111.	I am drawn to people suffering physical, emotional, or spiritual pain.
112.	When I pray for someone's healing, I do not put limits or restrictions on how God might work in that person's life (I do not believe that a physical healing miracle is the only answer to prayer).
113.	I know when people are speaking by the power of God's Holy Spirit.
114.	I see and understand the connections between the Old and New Testaments.
115.	Being thanked is not important to me; I serve regardless of recognition.
116.	It is important to me to introduce others to God and Jesus Christ.
117.	I am more interested in meeting people's physical needs than their spiritual needs.
118.	People seek out my opinion and advice on personal matters.
119.	I can speak (or sign) a language that I never formally studied.
120.	I am accepting of thoughts, beliefs, and behaviors of other people even when they are contrary to my own.
121.	I have a clear sense of the choices other people should make.
122.	My intuitions are strong, clear, and correct.
123.	I work best under pressure.
124.	I would like to represent the church in a foreign country.
125.	When Christians lose faith, it is my responsibility to try to help them recover it.
126.	Others tell me that I have a strong faith.
127.	When I pray, I petition God to change present circumstances.
128.	I speak the truth, even when what I say is unpopular or divisive.
129.	In groups, I emerge as a leader.
130.	My money management skills are of value to a church or group.
131.	I look for people who are suffering to offer my help to them.

132.	Others have told me that I have a healing touch or presence.
133.	I am deeply troubled by spiritual teachings that lack a solid theological or biblical basis.
134.	I am energized and excited when I teach others.
135.	I enjoy making work easier for other people.
136.	It is easy for me to extend an invitation to others to make a commitment to Christ.
137.	I prefer *doing* a job to *planning* a job.
138.	Others tell me that I am a good listener and counselor.
139.	I am able to communicate my faith and beliefs to people who speak other languages.
140.	I feel a kinship and connection to people of other faiths and cultures.
141.	When I am faced with hard life decisions, I turn to the Bible for guidance.
142.	I can sense when people are upset or angry, no matter how well they try to hide their feelings.
143.	I am a good judge of other people's gifts, skills, and passions for ministry and service.
144.	I want to learn a new language to enable me to be in ministry in a foreign land.
145.	I enjoy working with those who are new to the Christian faith.
146.	I see the image of God in every person I meet.
147.	I believe prayer yields tangible results, not just a good feeling or spiritual satisfaction.
148.	I talk to people about their beliefs concerning salvation, the afterlife, and God's will.
149.	I like directing and leading projects better than participating in them.
150.	My financial giving is anonymous.
151.	I reach out to people who are in trouble.
152.	When I see people in pain, I immediately pray for them.
153.	I know when a person is being dishonest.
154.	I would rather read scripture or theology than inspirational stories or Christian fiction.
155.	I like having a task defined for me rather than having to figure out a task for myself.
156.	I tell people what Christ has done in my life.
157.	I will do what I believe is right, even if it means that I have to break the rules.
158.	I challenge people with hard truths and discomforting information, even when it makes me unpopular.
159.	I am called to share my faith with other cultures, races, and faith traditions.
160.	I have the ability to automatically translate or interpret foreign words and phrases.
161.	God allows me to see the world from God's own perspective.
162.	I am able to apply difficult biblical concepts to real-world situations.
163.	I encourage others to use their gifts and talents to serve people beyond the church.

164.	I seek the opportunity to share the gospel with those outside the Christian faith or those who have not heard it before.
165.	I guide others in their discipleship journey and spiritual growth.
166.	I find that God's promises in the Bible have widespread validity in today's world.
167.	I help others see the miraculous in ordinary, everyday experiences.
168.	The Bible speaks directly to the political, economic, and justice issues of our day.
169.	People say that I am well organized.
170.	There is no limit to what I am willing to give to or do for others.
171.	I am very sensitive to the feelings of others.
172.	I encourage people to pray for the sick or afflicted.
173.	I find inspirational and spiritual meaning in secular books, films, speeches, and programs.
174.	I primarily read the Bible to learn and understand God's will.
175.	I prefer following to leading.
176.	I invite others to become active in a Christian faith community.
177.	I enjoy doing jobs that other people consider less important.
178.	I am first to offer an encouraging or supportive word to others.
179.	I have spoken a language without knowing what it was.
180.	I am able to share complex theological ideas with people of other races, cultures, and backgrounds.
181.	People tell me they are impressed by my insights.
182.	I look at issues from as many different points of view as possible.
183.	I enjoy organizing and managing human and material resources to accomplish a goal.
184.	I study other cultures and traditions to more effectively relate to people who are different from me.
185.	I want to get to know the people I serve and care for.
186.	Even when I grow discouraged, I never doubt or lack trust in God.
187.	My first reaction to problems or difficulties is to pray.
188.	I believe that God speaks through me.
189.	I experience God more in day-to-day living than in prayer, Bible reading, or going to church.
190.	I am prepared to give financial support to, or help raise funds for, any cause I believe in.
191.	Physical touch or the laying on of hands is an important part of spiritual healing.

192.	My faith is made strong by the miracles of God I witness in our world.
193.	I am able to help people gain a clearer understanding of God and the Bible.
194.	I enjoy creating lessons, resources, and tools for studying and discussing the Bible and the Christian faith.
195.	I make sure preparations are made so that meetings, programs, services, and projects run as smoothly as possible.
196.	I am more effective sharing my faith one-on-one than in front of a large group or crowd.
197.	My ministry is in my actions and behaviors more than in my words.
198.	I help people develop spiritual practices and disciplines that build their faith.
199.	People who speak other languages have little trouble communicating with me.
200.	I feel that God is leading me to involvement with other cultures, races, generations, and backgrounds.

Inventory Key

1. Wisdom
2. Knowledge
3. Administration
4. Apostleship
5. Shepherding   *3 —*
6. Faith   *2*
7. Miracles
8. Prophecy
9. Leadership
10. Giving

3 — 11. Compassion
12. Healing
13. Discernment
14. Teaching
15. Helping/Assistance
1* 16. Evangelism
17. Servanthood
18. Exhortation
19. Tongues
20. Interpretation of Tongues

Spiritual Gifts Inventory

Score Sheet

	7–ALWAYS	6–ALMOST ALWAYS	5–OFTEN	4–SOMETIMES	3–RARELY	2–ALMOST NEVER	1–NEVER			Total
1	1: 5	21: 5	41: 5	61: 7	81: 7	101: 5	121: 6	141: 7	161: 6	181: 5	58
2	2: 5	22: 7	42: 7	62: 7	82: 7	102: 7	122: 5	142: 7	162: 5	182: 5	62
3	3: 5	23: 7	43: 5	63: 5	83: 5	103: 5	123: 5	143: 5	163: 5	183: 1	48
4	4: 7	24: 7	44: 5	64: 7	84: 7	104: 1	124: 5	144: 5	164: 7	184: 3	54
5	5: 7	25: 7	45: 7	65: 7	85: 6	105: 7	125: 7	145: 7	165: 5	185: 7	67
6	6: 7	26: 7	46: 7	66: 7	86: 7	106: 5	126: 7	146: 7	166: 7	186: 7	68
7	7: 7	27: 7	47: 7	67: 7	87: 7	107: 7	127: 7	147: 7	167: 7	187: 5	68
8	8: 7	28: 6	48: 7	68: 7	88: 7	108: 7	128: 6	148: 7	168: 5	188: 7	66
9	9: 5	29: 7	49: 5	69: 5	89: 5	109: 7	129: 5	149: 5	169: 5	189: 3	52
10	10: 7	30: 5	50: 7	70: 5	90: 5	110: 7	130: 5	150: 5	170: 7	190: 7	55
11	11: 7	31: 7	51: 7	71: 6	91: 7	111: 5	131: 7	151: 7	171: 7	191: 7	67
12	12: 7	32: 7	52: 7	72: 7	92: 5	112: 7	132: 5	152: 7	172: 7	192: 7	66
13	13: 7	33: 5	53: 7	73: 7	93: 7	113: 7	133: 7	153: 7	173: 1	193: 5	60
14	14: 7	34: 7	54: 7	74: 5	94: 7	114: 7	134: 7	154: 5	174: 6	194: 4	62
15	15: 5	35: 7	55: 7	75: 5	95: 7	115: 7	135: 7	155: 5	175: 6	195: 7	63
16	16: 7	36: 7	56: 7	76: 7	96: 7	116: 7	136: 7	156: 7	176: 7	196: 7	70
17	17: 7	37: 7	57: 6	77: 7	97: 7	117: 1	137: 5	157: 5	177: 7	197: 5	57
18	18: 7	38: 7	58: 7	78: 5	98: 5	118: 5	138: 5	158: 6	178: 5	198: 6	58
19	19: 1	39: 1	59: 5	79: 5	99: 5	119: 1	139: 1	159: 1	179: 1	199: 2	24
20	20: 1	40: 1	60: 5	80: 5	100: 1	120: 5	140: 5	160: 1	180: 1	200: 3	28

Note: Your group leader will explain how to complete the score sheet and use the inventory key.

Definitions

Administration—the gift of organizing human and material resources for the work of Christ, including the ability to plan and work with people to delegate responsibilities, track progress, and evaluate the effectiveness of procedures. Administrators attend to details, communicate effectively, and take as much pleasure in working behind the scenes as they do in standing in the spotlight.

Apostleship—the gift of spreading the gospel of Jesus Christ to other cultures and to foreign lands. Apostleship is the missionary zeal that moves us from the familiar into uncharted territory to share the good news. Apostles embrace opportunities to learn foreign languages, visit other cultures, and go to places where people have not had the opportunity to hear the Christian message. The United States of America is fast becoming a mission field of many languages and cultures. It is no longer necessary to cross an ocean to enter the mission field. Even across generations, we may find that we need to "speak other languages" just to communicate.

Compassion—the gift of exceptional empathy with those in need that moves us to action. More than just concern, compassion demands that we share the suffering of others in order to connect the gospel truth with other realities of life. Compassion moves us beyond our comfort zones to offer practical, tangible aid to all God's children, regardless of the worthiness of the recipients or the response we receive for our service.

Discernment—the ability to separate truth from erroneous teachings and to rely on spiritual intuition to know what God is calling us to do. Discernment allows us to focus on what is truly important and to ignore that which deflects us from faithful obedience to God. Discernment aids us in knowing whom to listen to and whom to avoid.

Evangelism—the ability to share the gospel of Jesus Christ with those who have not heard it before or with those who have not yet made a decision for Christ. This gift is manifested in both one-on-one situations and in group settings, both large and small. Evangelism is an intimate relationship with another person or persons that requires the sharing of personal faith experience and a call for a response of faith to God.

Exhortation—the gift of exceptional encouragement. Exhorters see the silver lining in every cloud, offer deep and inspiring hope to the fellowship, and look for and commend the best in everyone. Exhorters empower others to feel good about themselves and to feel hopeful for the future. Exhorters are not concerned by appearances; they hold fast to what they know to be true and right and good.

Faith—the exceptional ability to hold fast to the truth of God in Jesus Christ in spite of pressures, problems, and obstacles to faithfulness. More than just belief, faith is a gift that empowers an individual or a group to hold fast to its identity in Christ in the face of any challenge. The gift of faith enables believers to rise above pressures and problems that might otherwise cripple them. Faith is characterized by an unshakable trust in God to deliver on God's promises, no matter what. The gift of faith inspires those who might be tempted to give up to hold on.

Giving—the gift of the ability to manage money to the honor and glory of God. Beyond the regular response of gratitude to God that all believers make, those with the gift of giving can discern the best ways to put money to work, can understand the validity and practicality of appeals for funds, and can guide others in the most faithful methods for managing their financial concerns.

Healing—the gift of conducting God's healing powers into the lives of God's people. Physical, emotional, spiritual, and psychological healing are all ways that healers manifest this gift. Healers are prayerful, and they help people understand that healing is in the hands of God. Often their task is to bring about such understanding more than it is to simply erase negative symptoms. Some of the most powerful healers display some of the most heartbreaking afflictions themselves.

Helping—the gift of making sure that everything is ready for the work of Christ to occur. Helpers assist others to accomplish the work of God. These unsung heroes work behind the scenes and attend to details that others would rather not be bothered with. Helpers function faithfully, regardless of the credit or attention they receive. Helpers provide the framework upon which the ministry of the body of Christ is built.

Interpretation of Tongues (see also Tongues)—the gift of (1) the ability to interpret foreign languages without the necessity of formal study in order to communicate with those who have not heard the Christian message or who seek to understand, or (2) the ability to interpret the gift of tongues as a secret prayer language that communicates with God at a deep spiritual level. Both understandings of the gift of interpretation of tongues are communal in nature: the first extends the good news into the world; the second strengthens the faith within the fellowship.

Knowledge—the gift of knowing the truth through faithful study of scripture and the human situation. Knowledge provides the information necessary for the transformation of the world and the formation of the body of Christ. Those possessing the gift of knowledge challenge the fellowship to improve itself through study, reading of scripture, discussion, and prayer.

Leadership—the gift of orchestrating the gifts and resources of others to accomplish the work of God. Leaders move people toward a God-given vision of service, and they enable others to use their gifts to the best of their abilities. Leaders are capable of creating synergy, whereby a group achieves much more than its individual members could achieve on their own.

Miracles—the gift of an ability to operate at a spiritual level that recognizes the miraculous work of God in the world. Miracle workers invoke God's power to accomplish that which appears impossible or impractical by worldly standards. Miracle workers remind us of the extraordinary nature of the ordinary world, thereby increasing faithfulness and trust in God. Miracle workers pray for God to work in the lives of others, and they feel no sense of surprise when their prayers are answered.

Prophecy—the gift of speaking the word of God clearly and faithfully. Prophets allow God to speak through them to communicate the message that people most need to hear. While often unpopular, prophets are able to say what needs to be said because of the spiritual empowerment they receive. Prophets do not foretell the future, but they proclaim God's future by revealing God's perspective on our current reality.

Servanthood—the gift of serving the spiritual and material needs of other people. Servants understand their role in the body of Christ to be that of giving comfort and aid to all who are in need. Servants look to the needs of others rather than focusing on their own needs. To serve is to put faith into action; it is to treat others as if they were Jesus Christ. The gift of service extends our Christian love into the world.

Shepherding—the gift of guidance. Shepherds nurture others in the Christian faith and provide a mentoring relationship to those who are new to the faith. Displaying an unusual spiritual maturity, shepherds share from their experience and learning to facilitate the spiritual growth and development of others. Shepherds take individuals under their care and walk with them on their spiritual journeys. Many shepherds provide spiritual direction and guidance to a wide variety of believers.

Teaching—the gift of bringing scriptural and spiritual truths to others. More than just teaching Christian education classes, teachers witness to the truth of Jesus Christ in a variety of ways, and they help others to understand the complex realities of the Christian faith. Teachers are revealers. They shine the light of understanding into the darkness of doubt and ignorance. They open people to new truths, and they challenge people to be more in the future than they have been in the past.

Tongues (see also **Interpretation of Tongues**)—the gift of (1) the ability to communicate the gospel to other people in a foreign language without the benefit of having studied said language (see Acts 2:4) or (2) the ability to speak to God in a secret, unknown prayer language that can only be understood by a person possessing the gift of interpretation. The ability to speak in the language of another culture makes the gift of tongues valuable for spreading the gospel throughout the world, while the gift of speaking a secret prayer language offers the opportunity to build faithfulness within a community of faith.

Wisdom—the gift of translating life experience into spiritual truth and of seeing the application of scriptural truth to daily living. The wise in our faith communities offer balance and understanding that transcend reason. Wisdom applies a God-given common sense to our understanding of God's will. Wisdom helps us remain focused on the important work of God, and it enables newer, less mature Christians to benefit from those who have been blessed by God to share deep truths.